HERSHEY'S

1934 *Cookbook*

HERSHEY'S

1934 *Cookbook*

Revised and expanded with chocolate recipes
brought up to date for use in today's kitchen

SMITHMARK

This edition published in 1999 by SMITHMARK Publishers,
a division of U.S. Media Holdings, Inc.,
115 West 18th Street, New York, NY 10011

Produced for SMITHMARK Publishers by
RD Publishing Services
Reader's Digest Road, Pleasantville, NY 10570-7000

All recipes developed and tested in the Hershey Kitchens.
Remember When text by Joshua Gaspero.
Designed by Marjorie Anderson.
Photographs on pages 22, 29, 32, 45, 52, 60, 63, 66, 70, 80, 98, and 102 by
Bob Skalkowski. Prop styling for these photographs by Richard H. Bach.
Photographs on pages 8 and 10–17: THE BETTMANN ARCHIVE.

ISBN: 0-7651-1741-X

10 9 8 7 6 5 4 3 2 1

SMITHMARK books are available for bulk purchase for sales promotion
and premium use. For details, write or call the manager of special sales,
SMITHMARK Publishers, 115 West 18th Street, New York, NY 10011;
(212) 519-1300.

Contents

Cakes

Icings & Sauces

Cream Cheese Glaze 46
Creamy Chocolate Frosting 40
Creamy White Frosting 38
Creole Icing 37
Fluffy Vanilla Icing 42
Mocha Cocoa Frosting 36

Mocha Icing 38
Rich Cocoa Frosting 36
Sugar Glaze 43
Two–Tone Glaze 43
Vanilla Butter Icing 37
Vanilla Drizzle 42

Pies

Chocolate Cream Pie 50
Chocolate Raisin Pie 50
Cocoa Cream Pie 51
Chocolate Pie 51

Chocolate Brownie Pie 53
Chocolate Butterscotch Pie 53
Home Front Coconut Cream Pie 54
Our Gal Sundae Pie 55

Desserts

Baked Chocolate Rice Pudding 64
Chocolate Bavarian Cream 65
Chocolate Bread Pudding 61
Chocolate Butterscotch Pudding 61
Chocolate Cream Eclairs 72
Chocolate Custard Ice Cream 69
Chocolate Marshmallow Pudding 65
Chocolate Ice Cream 58
Chocolate Souffle 73
Cocoa Cream Tapioca 64

Cocoa Marble Gingerbread 59
Cocoa Meringue Cake 67
Fireside Steamed Pudding 71
Mocha Chocolate Marlow 67
Old–Fashioned Chocolate
Ice Cream 58
Orange Custard–Filled
Chocolate Roll 62
Quick Creamy Chocolate Pudding 69
Steamed Chocolate Pudding 59

Breads

Berry Loaf 81
Bridge Party Coffee Cake 78
Chocolate Chip Orange Muffins 81
Chocolate Dessert Waffles 76
Chocolate–Pecan Filled Braid 77
Chocolate Tea Bread 82

Mini Chip Harvest Ring 79
Nostalgia Date–Nut Loaves 76
Orange–Cocoa Afternoon Biscuits 79
Raisin–Nut Cocoa Bread 82
Spiced Cocoa Doughnuts 78
Walnut Kuchen 83

Cookies

Blue Ribbon Fruit Cookies 97
Carol's Chocolate Coconut Squares 86
Chocolate Almond Nuggets 97
Chocolate Brownies Deluxe 91
Chocolate Coconut Macaroons 87
Chocolate Date and Nut Bars 101
Chocolate Fruit Cookies 99
Chocolate Midgets 90
Chocolate Oatmeal Raisin Cookies 87
Chocolate Pecan Pie Bars 101
Chocolate Pinks 89

Chocolate Robins 89
Chocolate Sandwiches 95
Chocolate Syrup Brownies 90
Chocolatetown Chip Cookies 86
Chocolate Thumbprint Cookies 93
Chocolate Walnut Wheels 100
Cocoa Bread Crumb Cookies 99
Cocoa–Molasses Drop Cookies 103
Mini Chip Brownies 91
Mini Chip Sugar Cookies 103
Silk Stocking Almond Cookies 94

Candies

Angel Fudge 110
Chocolate Chip Nougat Log 114
Chocolate Chip–Peanut Butter
Fudge 117
Chocolate Coconut Balls 116
Chocolate Coconut Squares 109
Chocolate Log Cabin Roll 107
Chocolate Nut Clusters 109

Chocolate Pecan Pralines 107
Chocolate Peanut Butter Fudge 111
Chocolate Potato Candy 112
Chocolate Popcorn Balls 117
Chocolate Turkish Paste 111
Cocoa Rum Balls 116
Country Club Two–Story Fudge 106
Creamy Cocoa Taffy 112

Fudge Caramels 110

Beverages

Chocoberry Splash 123
Chocolate Malted Milk 125
Chocolate Pineapple Freeze 120
Chocolate Syrup Iced Chocolate 124
Cokomoko Float 120
Five O'Clock Whipped Chocolate 125
Frosted Chocolate Shake 120

Hot Cocoa 123
Hot Cocoa For A Crowd 124
Mocha Shake 123
Orange Chocolate Float 124
Rich Iced Chocolate 121
Royal Hot Chocolate 127
Spanish Chocolate 125

Remember When

The 1930's. A decade of mixed blessings. Herbert Hoover was about to vacate the White House to be replaced by President-elect Roosevelt. The population of the United States was approximately 123 million people, and 53 million of them still lived on farms. Unemployment was creeping upwards to 25% of the labor force and, for those who worked, the hourly wage was 44¢. Economically we were in one of the worst periods of our lives, politically we were in a turmoil, and socially we looked about for any panacea that would temporarily remove our fears.

The Early 1930's

Life in the United States in the early 1930's was in a state of chaos, but the optimistic American remained dedicated to the hope that "things would get better." In the interim, it was necessary to "make do" while waiting for prosperity to come from "just around the corner." For one-third of the nation, necessities meant food, shelter and a job; for the remaining two-thirds it meant a home, meat on the table, a car, a radio and a regular Saturday night trip to the movies. After the movies, it might have meant a jaunt to a local tavern. Although prohibition had been in effect for 13 years, the absolute curtailment of an established social custom was just too unwieldy to enforce. In the early 1930's, prohibition was to have run its course, and the 18th Amendment was about to be repealed, ushered along with the tune of "Happy Days Are Here Again." For the Government, repeal of the 18th Amendment was a necessity needed to generate revenue for the Federal coffers. For the average American, repeal served as an indicator that things were possibly getting better in the home.

The home in the early 1930's ranged anywhere from a two room walk-up, with running water and sporadic coal heating, to a rambling 5-bedroom Victorian, that was passed down through the family. For the most part, however, the average home consisted of 6 rooms, a bath, a one-car detached garage, at a cost of around $2,500. Even though the garage came with the house, it may or may not have contained an automobile. If it did, it was anything from a 1925 Chevrolet that was five years old and had cost $825 new, to a 1930 Ford coupe that cost $600. America in 1930 was tightening her purse strings, and a new car every other year was considered luxury for only the very rich. The garages in many homes, in fact, garaged no car at all and masqueraded as a food cellar for home-jarred fruits and vegetables. Preparing and preserving peaches, cherries, pears and string beans was done not only for the pleasure it gave the homemaker, but because "store-bought" fruits and vegetables were becoming much too expensive. If the garage was not used as a pantry for home-prepared foods, it was, in dire extremes, used as an extra bedroom and a place to sleep for "Uncle Louis who was laid off his job in the automobile factory in Detroit." An ironic fate in an ironic era.

The living room of the American home at the beginning of the decade with its large easy chairs, high-back sofas with doilies on the arm rest and antimacassars on the back, slightly worn rugs and colored prints on the wall were all accouterments to the mainstay of American family life, the radio. Radios in the 30's ranged from a small console ($19.95) to an "Oxford Hepplewhite de luxe highboy with sliding doors, American walnut finish with Australian lacewood paneling" ($150, not counting tubes; Western prices slightly higher). Through the brown box in the living room came the voices of "Amos 'n' Andy" in their nightly 15-minute sketch (Monday-Friday 7:00 EST NBC Red Network), the melodic chirps of the "Songbird of the South," Kate Smith ("Hello Everybody") and the voice of the adventurous Lowell Thomas. The radio, indeed, commanded an incredible audience. It was everyone's passkey to adventure, music, laughter and news at least five nights a week.

On a Saturday night it was typical for most Americans to take leave from their radios in the living room and further escape into the celluloid realm of Hollywood. In the 1930's an estimated 60-million people weekly walked, rode and ran to the neighborhood Bijou, Orpheum or Rex, paid their admission (adults 25¢, children 10¢) and watched with total involvement the plights and romances of their cinematic idols. In the 30's you could hear your idols talk, sing, yell and cry, with an appropriate background of canned music. Gone were the titled screens, and gone were the theater orchestras, a situation loudly declaimed by the American Federation of Musicians ("I went to the Canned Goods Fair, the prunes and the tunes were there..."). Though of poor quality, sound was in, and so were the idols it created. Clark Gable, Will Rogers, Janet Gaynor, Joan Crawford, Norma Shearer, Wallace Beery, Mae West, W. C. Fields were all familiar names to moviegoers. When they died a tragic death or lost a forlorn lover, the audience in the

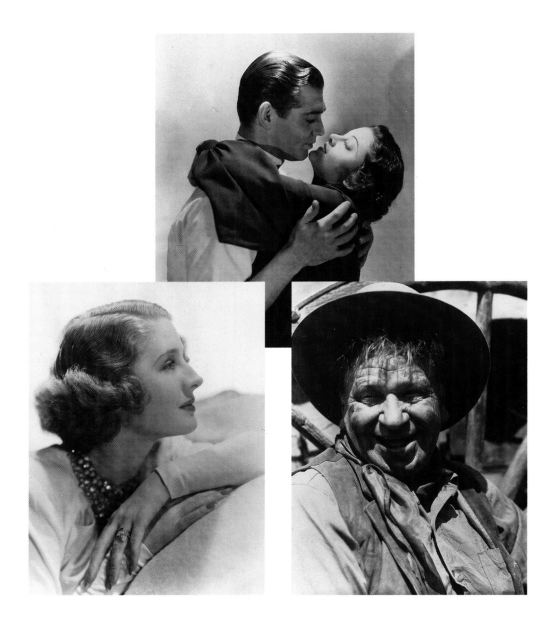

moment was totally empathetic, an empathy that somehow overshadowed the trouble of their own lives. Besides the escapism that movies offered, they sometimes offered more tangible rewards. The era of the "talkies" was the era of the promotion. Giveaways at local theaters ("Dish night: Collect a complete set of fine dinnerware completely free") hastened the return of moviegoers week after week. No matter that it took at least a year to collect a complete set, it was free and anything that was free in the 1930's received a warm welcome. Almost as warm a welcome as the Sunday papers and the comic adventures of the rotogravured heroes who inhabited them.

The most popular reading matter of the day was by far the Sunday comics. In spite of the success of the *Literary Digest, Vanity Fair,* the *Saturday Evening Post, The American Mercury* and *Liberty Magazine* ("reading time 12 minutes 35 seconds"), they were all overshadowed in the average home by Little Orphan Annie ("Arf" says Sandy) and her Sunday sidekicks. Dick Tracy, Gasoline Alley, Maggie & Jiggs and a host of others warmed the hearts of Americans in the 1930's, first in the comics and later in radio, novels and Big-Little Books. America's heroes may have been on paper, but to the reading audience they were real, a curiosity which sometimes diminished the problems of the times and most of all the problems of the American housewife.

The American housewife in the 1930's, with the economy the way it was, had an extremely difficult job. She was expected to make do for her family in times when there was little or no money coming in. Economy and thrift were the watch words of the day. All the everyday purchases, whether for dinner, cleaning, dressing or general housework, were made with eye on the pocketbook. Meals were planned around the general staple sold by the local butcher and baker and with vegetables and fruits that were canned at home. (In the 1930's sirloin steak sold for

29¢ a pound, bacon was 11¢ a pound, potatoes were 2¢ a pound and bread was 5¢ a loaf.) Soup, selling at 12¢ a can and serving four, augmented many a meal. Soup with her own vegetables added, in many instances, was the meal. For the most part, keeping the house clean was a manual job done with polish, yellow soap and a lot of elbow grease. Keeping the insects away was done with Flit ("quick, Henry, the Flit"). Carpet sweepers cleaned the rugs in as much as vacuum cleaners complete with attachments were still a little bit too expensive. (A 1932 Hoover, with attachments, sold for $79.50.) The wash was generally done in an electric washing machine ($47.95) and, although a welcome replacement for the scrub board, it took its toll in many a finger caught in the wringer. The homemaker, with all her other chores, was also a "cottage industry" in terms of clothing for the family. Although the sewing machine (the Singer with the treadle) was an expensive purchase, it more than paid for itself in terms of clothes, clothes that were worn and then passed down to a younger brother or sister.

The kitchen of the American home of the 1930's was the domain of the housewife. Besides being a place for preparation and preserving, it was also the place where countless hours were spent baking. Cookies, cakes pies, icings and frostings were made—and "from scratch" (an event of much pleasure to younger members of the family who got to lick the mixing bowl). Mixing was done with either an electric mixer ($9.95), or more popularly with an egg beater, a bowl and spoon. All the natural ingredients were used (butter was 28¢ a pound, milk 10¢ a quart, eggs were 29¢ a dozen and sugar was 5¢ a pound). When she baked with chocolate, more often than not, she used HERSHEY'S chocolate products. In the 1930's the Hershey Chocolate Company was making products for baking, as it had been for some 30 years. Cocoa, Baking Chocolate, Chocolate Syrup and Milk Chocolate Bars were all to be found in the kitchen of almost every American home. Recipes were original, passed down for generations, or gleaned from a Hershey Chocolate Cookbook. No matter what the source, the finished products were the best ever made, and nobody could bake like your mother. Except for you, when you turn these pages.

Cakes

Demon Cake (page 20)

DEMON CAKE

4 bars (4 oz.) HERSHEY'S
  Unsweetened Baking Chocolate
1 cup (2 sticks) butter, softened
2¼ cups sugar
5 eggs, separated
2¾ cups cake flour
1 teaspoon baking soda

½ teaspoon baking powder
½ teaspoon salt
1½ cups buttermilk or sour
  milk
1 teaspoon vanilla extract
Fluffy Vanilla Icing (page 42)

Heat oven to 350°F. Grease and flour three 9-inch round baking pans. In top of double boiler over hot, not boiling, water melt chocolate. Set aside to cool slightly. In large mixer bowl, beat butter and sugar until light and fluffy. Add chocolate; beat until blended. Add egg yolks; beat well. Stir together flour baking soda, baking powder and salt; add alternately with buttermilk and vanilla to butter mixture, beating until well blended. Beat egg whites until stiff, but not dry; fold into batter. Pour batter into prepared pans. Bake 30 to 35 minutes or until wooden pick inserted in center comes out clean. Cool 10 minutes; remove from pans to wire racks. Cool completely. Frost with Fluffy Vanilla Icing.

Yield: 10 to 12 servings.

THREE LAYER GOLD CAKE

½ cup (1 stick) butter, softened
½ cup shortening
1½ cups granulated sugar
1 cup powdered sugar
2 teaspoons vanilla extract
5 eggs, separated

2⅔ cups all-purpose flour
3 teaspoons baking powder
½ teaspoon salt
1¼ cups milk
Rich Cocoa Frosting (page 36)

Heat oven to 350°F. Grease and flour three 9-inch round baking pans. In large mixer bowl, beat butter, shortening, granulated sugar, powdered sugar and vanilla until creamy. Add egg yolks; beat well. Stir together flour, baking powder and salt; add alternately with milk to butter mixture, beating well after each addition. In small mixer bowl, beat egg whites until stiff; fold into batter. Pour batter into prepared pans. Bake 25 to 30 minutes or until wooden pick inserted in center comes out clean. Cool 10 minutes; remove from pans to wire racks. Cool completely. Frost with Rich Cocoa Frosting.

Yield: 10 to 12 servings.

UPSIDE-DOWN CHOCOLATE CAKE

2 tablespoons plus ⅓ cup butter
½ cup packed light brown sugar
1 can (1 lb.) apricot halves,
    drained
8 to 10 maraschino cherries,
    halved
¾ cup granulated sugar

¼ cup HERSHEY'S Cocoa
Dash ground cinnamon
2 eggs
1¾ cups cake flour
1 teaspoon baking soda
¾ cup milk
½ teaspoon vanilla extract

Heat oven to 350°F. In 9-inch square baking pan, melt 2 tablespoons butter in oven. Remove from oven. Stir in brown sugar. Arrange apricot halves, rounded side down, and cherries in the pan. Set aside. In small mixer bowl, beat ⅓ cup butter and granulated sugar until light and fluffy. Add cocoa and cinnamon; beat until blended. Add eggs; beat well. Stir together flour and baking soda; add alternately with milk to cocoa mixture, beating until well blended. Stir in vanilla. Pour batter into pan over fruit. Bake 45 to 50 minutes or until wooden pick inserted in center comes out clean. With metal spatula, loosen sides; invert cake onto serving plate. Serve warm.
    Yield: 8 servings.

COCOA POTATO CAKE

½ cup (1 stick) butter, softened
2 cups sugar
3 eggs, separated
1 cup hot mashed potatoes
2 cups all-purpose flour
½ cup HERSHEY'S Cocoa

2 teaspoons baking powder
Dash ground cinnamon
½ cup milk
½ teaspoon vanilla exract
½ cup chopped nuts
Chocolate Nut Icing (page 40)

Heat oven to 350°F. Grease and flour 13 x 9 x 2-inch baking pan. In large mixer bowl, beat butter and sugar until light and fluffy. Add egg yolks, one at a time, beating well after each addition. Gradually add mashed potatoes, beating until well blended. Stir together flour, cocoa, baking powder and cinnamon; add alternately with milk to butter mixture. Stir in vanilla and nuts. In small mixer bowl, beat egg whites until stiff peaks form; fold into chocolate batter. Pour batter into prepared pan. Bake 35 to 40 minutes or until wooden pick inserted in center comes out clean. Cool cake in pan on wire rack. Frost with Chocolate Nut Icing.
    Yield: 12 to 15 servings.

CHICAGO FUDGE CAKE

3 bars (3 oz.) HERSHEY'S
   Unsweetened Baking Chocolate
½ cup (1 stick) butter, softened
2 cups packed light brown sugar
2 eggs, separated
1 teaspoon vanilla extract
2⅓ cups cake flour
1 teaspoon baking soda

½ teaspoon salt
½ cup sour milk
½ cup water
¼ teaspoon ground cinnamon
⅓ cup chopped raisins
¼ cup chopped nuts
Creamy White Frosting (page 38)

Heat oven to 350°F. Line bottoms of three 8-inch round baking pans with wax paper. In top of double boiler over hot, not boiling, water melt chocolate; set aside. In large mixer bowl, beat butter and brown sugar until creamy. Add egg yolks and vanilla; beat well. Stir together flour, baking soda and salt; add alternately with sour milk and water to butter mixture, beating until blended. In small mixer bowl, beat egg whites until stiff peaks form; fold into butter mixture. Remove 1½ cups batter; into that batter stir cinnamon, raisins and nuts. Pour batter into one prepared pan. Stir chocolate into remaining batter; pour batter into remaining two prepared pans. Bake all layers 30 to 35 minutes or until wooden pick inserted in center comes out clean. Cool 10 minutes; remove from pans to wire racks. Carefully remove wax paper. Cool completely. Frost with Creamy White Frosting.

Yield: 10 to 12 servings.

SIMPLE COCOA LAYER CAKE

½ cup (1 stick) butter, softened
1¼ cups sugar
1 teaspoon vanilla extract
2 eggs, separated
2 cups all-purpose flour
½ cup HERSHEY'S Cocoa

1½ teaspoons baking powder
½ teaspoon baking soda
¼ teaspoon salt
1¼ cups milk
Busy Day Cocoa Icing (page 39)

Heat oven to 350°F. Grease and flour two 8-inch round baking pans. In large mixer bowl, beat butter, sugar and vanilla until creamy. Add egg yolks; beat well. Stir together flour, cocoa, baking powder, baking soda and salt; add alternately with milk to butter mixture. In small mixer bowl, beat egg whites until stiff peaks form; fold into batter. Pour batter into prepared pans. Bake 30 to 35 minutes or until wooden pick inserted in center comes out clean. Cool 10 minutes; remove from pans to wire racks. Cool completely. Frost with Busy Day Cocoa Icing.

Yield: 8 to 10 servings.

OLD–FASHIONED COCOA MINT CAKE

¾ cup (1½ sticks) butter,
  softened
1⅔ cups sugar
3 eggs
2 cups all-purpose flour
⅔ cup HERSHEY'S Cocoa
1¼ teaspoons baking soda

1 teaspoon salt
¼ teaspoon baking powder
1⅓ cups water
½ cup crushed hard peppermint
  candy
Cocoa Peppermint Icing
  (page 40)

Heat oven to 350°F. Grease and flour two 9-inch round baking pans. In large mixer bowl, beat butter, sugar and eggs until fluffy. Continue to beat vigorously 3 minutes (high speed of mixer). Stir together flour, cocoa, baking soda, salt and baking powder; add alternately with water to butter mixture. Blend just until combined; stir in candy. Pour batter into prepared pans. Bake 30 to 35 minutes or until wooden pick inserted in center comes out clean. Cool 10 minutes; remove from pans to wire racks. Cool completely. Frost with Cocoa Peppermint Icing.

Yield: 8 to 10 servings.

Old–Fashioned Cocoa Mint Cake, Hershey's Special Cake; Chocolate Crumb Cake

CHOCOLATE CRUMB CAKE

2 cups all-purpose flour
1 cup sugar
1½ teaspoons baking soda
½ teaspoon baking powder
¼ teaspoon salt

¼ cup (½ stick) butter, softened
1 egg
¾ cup milk
½ cup (5½ oz. can) HERSHEY'S
   Syrup

Heat oven to 350°F. Grease 9-inch square baking pan. In large mixer bowl, stir together flour and sugar. Remove ½ cup mixture; set aside for topping. Stir baking soda, baking powder and salt into remaining flour mixture. Add butter, egg, milk and syrup; beat until well blended. Pour batter into prepared pan. Sprinkle reserved flour mixture over top. Bake 30 to 35 minutes or until wooden pick inserted in center comes out clean. Serve warm or at room temperature.

Yield: 6 to 9 servings.

HERSHEY'S SPECIAL CAKE

3 bars (3 oz.) HERSHEY'S
   Unsweetened Baking Chocolate
½ cup (1 stick) butter, softened
1½ cups sugar
2 eggs
½ teaspoon salt

2 cups cake flour or 1¾ cups
   all-purpose flour
1 cup sour milk
1 teaspoon baking soda
1 tablespoon white vinegar
Chocolate Frosting (page 42)

Heat oven to 375°F. Grease and flour two 9-inch round baking pans. In top of double boiler over hot, not boiling, water melt chocolate. Set aside to cool slightly. In large mixer bowl, beat butter and sugar until light and fluffy. Add eggs, one at a time, beating well after each addition. Stir together flour and salt; add alternately with milk to butter mixture, beating until well blended. Add chocolate; beat until blended. In small cup, combine baking soda and vinegar, stirring until baking soda is dissolved. Add to batter; beat until blended. Pour batter into prepared pans. Bake 25 to 30 minutes or until wooden pick inserted in center comes out clean. Cool 10 minutes; remove from pans to wire racks. Cool completely. Frost with Chocolate Frosting.

Yield: 8 to 10 servings.

OLD–FASHIONED CHOCOLATE CAKE

4½ bars (4 ½ oz.)
  HERSHEY'S Unsweetened
  Baking Chocolate
½ cup water
¾ cup (1½ sticks) butter,
  softened
2¼ cups sugar

6 eggs, separated
1½ teaspoons vanilla extract
2⅔ cups cake flour
3 teaspoons baking powder
¾ teaspoon salt
¾ cup milk

Heat oven to 350°F. Grease and flour 13 x 9 x 2-inch baking pan. In top of double boiler over hot, not boiling, water melt chocolate with water. Set aside to cool slightly. In large mixer bowl, beat butter and sugar until light and fluffy. Add egg yolks and vanilla; beat well. Add chocolate; beat until blended. Stir together flour, baking powder and salt; add alternately with milk to butter mixture. In small mixer bowl, beat egg whites until stiff; fold into batter. Pour batter into prepared pan. Bake 45 to 50 minutes or until wooden pick inserted in center comes out clean. Cool in pan on wire rack. Frost as desired.
   Yield: 12 to 15 servings.

DEVIL'S DELIGHT CAKE

4 bars (4 oz.) HERSHEY'S
  Unsweetened Baking Chocolate
1 ⅔ cups packed light brown
  sugar, divided
1½ cups milk, divided
3 eggs, separated

⅓ cup butter, softened
2 cups cake flour
1 teaspoon baking soda
¼ teaspoon salt
1 teaspoon vanilla extract

Heat oven to 350°F. Grease and flour two 9-inch round baking pans. In top of double boiler over hot, not boiling, water melt chocolate. Add ⅔ cup brown sugar, 1 cup milk and 1 slightly beaten egg yolk. Cook, stirring constantly with wire whisk, until well blended. Remove from heat; cool slightly. In large mixer bowl, beat butter until creamy; add ½ cup brown sugar, beating until well blended. Add remaining 2 egg yolks; beat well. Stir together flour, baking soda and salt; add to butter mixture alternately with remaining ½ cup milk, beating until well blended. Add chocolate mixture and vanilla; beat until blended. In small mixer bowl, beat egg whites until foamy; gradually add remaining ½ cup brown sugar, beating until stiff peaks form. Fold into chocolate batter; pour into prepared pans. Bake 30 to 35 minutes or until wooden pick inserted in center comes out clean. Cool 10 minutes; remove pans to wire racks. Cool completely. Frost as desired.
   Yield : 8 to 10 servings.

CREOLE CHOCOLATE CAKE

3 bars (3 oz.) HERSHEY'S
   Unsweetened Baking Chocolate
1½ cups sugar, divided
1 cup milk
4 eggs
½ cup (1 stick) butter, softened

1 teaspoon vanilla extract
2 cups all-purpose flour
1 tablespoon baking powder
Dash ground cinnamon
Creole Icing (page 37)

Heat oven to 350°F. Grease and flour two 9-inch round baking pans. In top of double boiler over hot, not boiling water, melt chocolate. Add ½ cup sugar and milk; cook, stirring constantly, until well blended. Remove from heat; gradually add 1 well-beaten egg, stirring until blended. Set aside to cool. In large mixer bowl, beat butter and remaining 1 cup sugar until light and fluffy. Add remaining 3 eggs and vanilla; beat well. Add chocolate mixture; beat until blended. Stir together flour, baking powder and cinnamon; gradually add to butter mixture, beating until blended. Pour batter into prepared pans. Bake 25 to 30 minutes or until wooden pick inserted in center comes out clean. Cool 10 minutes; remove from pans to wire racks. Cool completely. Frost with Creole Icing.

Yield: 10 to 12 servings.

MARBLE CAKE

2 bars (2 oz.) HERSHEY'S
   Unsweetened Baking Chocolate
1¼ cups (2½ sticks) butter,
   softened
3 cups sugar
1½ teaspoons vanilla extract

3⅓ cups cake flour
3¾ teaspoons baking powder
1½ cups milk
5 egg whites
Vanilla Butter Icing (page 37)
Chocolate Glaze (page 43)

Heat oven to 350°F. Grease and flour 13 x 9 x 2-inch baking pan. In top of double boiler over hot, not boiling, water melt chocolate. Set aside to cool slightly. In large mixer bowl, beat butter, sugar and vanilla until light and fluffy. Stir together flour and baking powder; add alternately with milk to butter mixture, beating until well blended. In small mixer bowl, beat egg whites until stiff peaks form; gently fold into batter. Remove 1½ cups batter to separate bowl; stir chocolate into that batter. Spoon vanilla and chocolate batters alternately into prepared pan; swirl with metal spatula for marbled effect. Bake 55 to 60 minutes or until wooden pick inserted in center comes out clean. Cool in pan on wire rack. Frost with double recipe Vanilla Butter Icing. Drizzle Chocolate Glaze over top; allow to set.

Yield: 12 to 15 servings

COFFEE CHOCOLATE CAKE

4 bars (4 oz.) HERSHEY'S
   Unsweetened Baking Chocolate
2 egg yolks
1 cup sour milk
½ cup (1 stick) butter, softened
2 cups packed light brown sugar
1 teaspoon vanilla extract

3½ cups all-purpose flour
1 teaspoon baking powder
1 teaspoon baking soda
½ teaspoon salt
1 cup brewed coffee
Chocolate Butter Filling (page 39)
Chocolate Butter Icing (page 37)

Heat oven to 350°F. Grease and flour two 9-inch round baking pans. In top of double boiler over hot, not boiling, water melt chocolate. In small bowl, beat egg yolks with milk until blended; gradually stir into chocolate. Cook, stirring constantly, until thickened. Set aside to cool. In large mixer bowl, beat butter, brown sugar and vanilla until well blended. Stir together flour, baking powder, baking soda and salt; add alternately with coffee to butter mixture, beating until well blended. Add chocolate mixture; beat until blended. Pour batter into prepared pans. Bake 30 to 35 minutes or until wooden pick inserted in center comes out clean. Cool 10 minutes; remove from pans to wire racks. Cool completely. To assemble, split each layer horizontally in half. Place first cake layer on large serving plate. Spread one-third of Chocolate Butter Filling on top of cake layer. Top with second layer; spread with one-third filling. Place third layer on top; spread on remaining filling. Top with remaining layer. Frost sides and top of cake with Chocolate Frosting.

Yield: 10 to 12 servings.

RED DEVIL'S FOOD CAKE

½ cup shortening
1¼ cups sugar
2 eggs
1 cup boiling water
½ cup HERSHEY'S Cocoa

1¾ cups cake flour or 1½ cups
   all-purpose flour
1 teaspoon baking soda
1 teaspoon salt
1 teaspoon vanilla extract

Heat oven to 350°F. Grease and flour two 8-inch round baking pans. In large mixer bowl, beat shortening and sugar until well blended; add eggs, one at a time, beating well after each addition. Add in order without stirring: water, cocoa, flour, baking soda, salt and vanilla. After all ingredients have been added, beat vigorously until smooth. Pour batter into prepared pans. Bake 30 to 35 minutes or until wooden pick inserted in center comes out clean. Cool 10 minutes; remove from pans to wire racks. Cool completely. Frost as desired.

Yield: 8 to 10 servings.

CHOCOLATE ICEBERG CUPCAKES

3 bars (3 oz.) HERSHEY'S
   Unsweetened Baking Chocolate
½ cup (1 stick) butter, softened
1 cup sugar
2 eggs, separated
2 cups cake flour
1½ teaspoons baking powder
¾ teaspoon baking soda
¼ teaspoon salt
⅔ cup milk
1 teaspoon vanilla extract
Vanilla Butter Icing (page 37)
Shredded coconut (optional)

Heat oven to 350°F. Paper-line muffin cups (2½ inches in diameter). In top of double boiler over hot, not boiling, water melt chocolate. Set aside to cool slightly. In large mixer bowl, beat butter and sugar until light and fluffy. Add egg yolks; beat well. Add chocolate; beat until blended. Stir together flour, baking powder, baking soda and salt; add alternately with milk to butter mixture, beating until well blended. Stir in vanilla. In small mixer bowl, beat egg whites until stiff; fold into batter. Fill prepared muffin cups half full with batter. Bake 15 to 20 minutes or until wooden pick inserted in center comes out clean. Remove from cups to wire racks. Cool completely. Frost with double recipe Vanilla Butter Icing. Sprinkle shredded coconut over top, if desired.

Yield: About 2½ dozen cupcakes.

FAVORITE POUND CAKE

½ cup (1 stick) butter, softened
½ cup shortening
2 cups sugar
4 eggs
½ teaspoon baking soda
1 cup buttermilk
3 cups all-purpose flour
¼ teaspoon salt
2 teaspoons lemon extract
1 teaspoon almond extract
Powdered sugar (optional)

Heat oven to 350°F. Grease and lightly flour 10-inch tube pan. In large mixer bowl, beat butter and shortening until blended. Gradually add sugar, beating until creamy. Add eggs, one at a time, beating well after each addition. Stir baking soda into buttermilk. Add flour and salt alternately with buttermilk mixture to butter mixture, beating just until blended. Stir in lemon and almond extracts. Pour batter into prepared pan. Bake 1 hour and 10 minutes or until wooden pick inserted comes out clean. Cool 15 minutes; remove from pan to wire rack. Cool completely. Sift powdered sugar over top, if desired.

Yield: 12 to 16 servings.

PARTY PINK CHOCOLATE CAKE ROLL

4 eggs, separated
½ cup plus ⅓ cup sugar
1 teaspoon vanilla extract
½ cup all-purpose flour
⅓ cup HERSHEY'S Cocoa
½ teaspoon baking powder
¼ teaspoon baking soda
⅛ teaspoon salt

⅓ cup water
Cherry Cream Filling:
  1½ cups cold whipping cream
  ½ cup powdered sugar
  1 teaspoon vanilla extract
  4 to 6 drops red food color
  ½ cup maraschino cherries,
    well drained and chopped

Heat oven to 375°F. Line 15½ x 10½ x 1-inch jelly roll pan with foil; generously grease foil. In large mixer bowl, beat egg whites until foamy; gradually add ½ cup sugar, beating until stiff peaks form. Set aside. In small mixer bowl, beat egg yolks and vanilla on high speed of electric mixer 3 minutes; gradually add remaining ⅓ cup sugar. Continue beating 2 additional minutes. Combine flour, cocoa, baking powder, baking soda and salt; add alternately with water to egg yolk mixture, beating on low speed just until batter is smooth. Gradually fold chocolate mixture into egg whites until blended. Spread batter evenly in prepared pan. Bake 12 to 15 minutes or until top springs back when touched lightly in center. Immediately loosen cake from edges of pan; invert on towel sprinkled with powdered sugar, Carefully remove foil. Immediately roll cake in towel starting from narrow end; place on wire rack to cool. Prepare Cherry Cream Filling. Unroll cake; remove towel. Spread about half of the filling over cake; reroll cake. Spread remaining filling over top and sides. Garnish with grated chocolate and maraschino cherries.

Cherry Cream Filling

In large mixer bowl, beat whipping cream, powdered sugar, vanilla and food color until stiff. Fold in maraschino cherries. *About 3 cups filling.*

Yield: 10 to 12 servings

Icings & Sauces

Chocolate Glaze *(page 43)*

CHOCOLATE ICING

2 bars (2 oz.) HERSHEY'S
 Unsweetened Baking Chocolate
¼ cup (½ stick) butter,
 softened

2 cups powdered sugar
1 teaspoon vanilla extract
3 tablespoons milk or light cream

In top of double boiler over hot, not boiling, water melt chocolate. In small mixer bowl, beat butter until creamy. Gradually add powdered sugar and vanilla, beating until blended. Add chocolate; beat well. Add milk, beating until of spreading consistency.

Yield: About 1⅓ cups.

MOCHA COCOA FROSTING

⅓ cup butter, softened
3 cups powdered sugar
½ cup HERSHEY'S Cocoa
¼ teaspoon salt

⅓ cup strong brewed coffee
½ teaspoon vanilla extract

In small mixer bowl, beat butter until creamy. stir together powdered sugar, cocoa and salt; add alternately with coffee and vanilla to butter, beating until smooth and of spreading consistency.

Yield: About 1¾ cups frosting.

RICH COCOA FROSTING

10 tablespoons butter, softened
2 tablespoons light corn syrup
1½ teaspoons vanilla extract
⅛ teaspoon salt

4 cups powdered sugar
1 cup HERSHEY'S Cocoa
½ cup milk

In large mixer bowl, beat butter, corn syrup, vanilla and salt until blended; add powdered sugar and cocoa alternately with milk, beating to spreading consistency.

Yield: About 3 cups frosting.

CREOLE ICING

3 tablespoons butter, softened
3¼ cups powdered sugar
3 tablespoons HERSHEY'S
   Cocoa

Dash ground cinnamon
¼ cup warm brewed coffee
1 tablespoon warm water
½ teaspoon vanilla extract

In small mixer bowl, beat butter until creamy. Add powdered sugar, cocoa and cinnamon alternately with coffee, water and vanilla; beat until of spreading consistency. (Add additional water, 1 teaspoon at a time, if necessary.)
Yield: About 1¾ cups.

VANILLA BUTTER ICING

3 tablespoons butter, softened
1½ cups powdered sugar
1 to 2 tablespoons milk

1½ teaspoons vanilla extract
4 drops red food color (optional)

In small mixer bowl, beat butter and sugar until light and fluffy; add milk and vanilla, beating until smooth and of spreading consistency.

Pink Butter Icing

Add red food color to Vanilla Butter Icing; stir until blended.

Yield: About ¾ cup.

CHOCOLATE BUTTER ICING

3 squares (3 oz.) HERSHEY'S
   Unsweetened Baking Chocolate
6 tablespoons butter, softened

1 cup powdered sugar
1 to 2 tablespoons light cream
1 teaspoon vanilla extract

In top of double boiler over hot, not boiling, water melt chocolate. In small mixer bowl, beat butter until creamy; gradually add powdered sugar, light cream and vanilla, beating until smooth. Add chocolate; beat to spreading consistency (add additional light cream, if necessary).
Yield: About 1¼ cups.

BITTER CHOCOLATE BUTTER ICING

4 bars (4 oz.) HERSHEY'S
   Unsweetened Baking Chocolate
½ cup (1 stick) butter, softened

2 cups powdered sugar
2 to 3 tablespoons light cream

In top of double boiler over hot, not boiling, water melt chocolate. Set aside to cool slightly. In small mixer bowl, beat butter until creamy. Add powdered sugar alternately with light cream, beating until well blended. Add chocolate; beat until of spreading consistency.

Yield: 2½ cups.

MOCHA ICING

5 tablespoons butter, softened
3 tablespoons HERSHEY'S
   Cocoa
2½ cups powdered sugar

3 tablespoons strong brewed
   coffee or 2 teaspoons powdered
   instant coffee dissolved in 3
   tablespoons hot water
1 teaspoon vanilla extract

In small mixer bowl, beat butter until creamy. Add cocoa; beat until blended. Add powdered sugar alternately with coffee, beating until smooth and of spreading consistency. Stir in vanilla.

Yield: About 1½ cups.

CREAMY WHITE FROSTING

1 cup shortening
½ cup (1 stick) butter, softened
6½ cups powdered sugar

½ cup whole milk
1 tablespoon vanilla extract

In large mixer bowl, beat shortening and butter until blended. Add powdered sugar alternately with milk and vanilla, beating until smooth and of spreading consistency.

Yield: About 5 cups frosting.

CHOCOLATE BUTTER FILLING

2 bars (2 oz.) HERSHEY'S
   Unsweetened Baking Chocolate
2 tablespoons butter, softened
1⅔ cups powdered sugar
3 tablespoons milk

½ teaspoon vanilla extract
⅓ cup cold whipping cream
¼ cup chopped nuts
¼ cup chopped maraschino
   cherries, well drained

In top of double boiler over hot, not boiling, water melt chocolate. Set aside to cool slightly. In small mixer bowl, beat butter and powdered sugar until well blended. Add chocolate, milk and vanilla; beat well. In separate bowl, beat whipping cream until stiff; fold into chocolate mixture. Fold in nuts and cherries. Spread filling between two baked and cooled chocolate or white cake layers. Frost top and sides of cake with desired frosting or with sweetened whipped cream.

Yield: About 1¾ cups filling.

BUSY DAY COCOA ICING

¼ cup (½ stick) butter, softened
6 tablespoons boiling water
½ cup HERSHEY'S Cocoa

2 teaspoons vanilla extract
3 cups powdered sugar

In small bowl, stir together butter and water until butter is melted. Add cocoa and vanilla; beat until well blended. Gradually add powdered sugar, beating until smooth and creamy and of spreading consistency. (Add additional water, if necessary.)

Yield: About 2 cups.

COCOA CREAM FILLING

2 tablespoons butter
¼ cup HERSHEY'S Cocoa
½ cup granulated sugar

⅓ cup light cream
¼ teaspoon vanilla extract
⅓ cup powdered sugar

In small saucepan over low heat, melt butter; add cocoa. Cook, stirring constantly, until thickened. Add granulated sugar and light cream; cook and stir until smooth. Remove from heat; stir in vanilla. Gradually add powdered sugar, stirring until well blended.

Yield: About ¾ cup filling.

COCOA PEPPERMINT ICING

½ cup (1 stick) butter
½ cup HERSHEY'S Cocoa
3⅔ cups (1 lb. box)
   powdered sugar

7 tablespoons milk
1 teaspoon vanilla extract
1 tablespoon crushed hard
   peppermint candy

In medium saucepan over low heat, melt butter; add cocoa, stirring until mixture is smooth and well blended. Remove from heat. Alternately add powdered sugar and milk, beating until of spreading consistency. Stir in vanilla and candy.

Yield: About 2¼ cups icing or enough for an 8- or 9- inch layer cake.

CHOCOLATE NUT ICING

¼ cup HERSHEY'S Cocoa
6 tablespoons boiling water
3 cups powdered sugar

½ teaspoon vanilla extract
½ cup chopped nuts

In medium bowl, stir together cocoa and water until smooth. Gradually add powdered sugar, beating until of spreading consistency. (Additional boiling water may be needed.) Stir in vanilla and nuts.

Yield: About 1½ cups or enough for top of 13 x 9 x 2-inch cake.

CREAMY CHOCOLATE FROSTING

2⅔ cups powdered sugar
¼ cup HERSHEY'S Cocoa
6 tablespoons butter, softened
1 teaspoon vanilla extract

1 tablespoon light corn syrup
   (optional)
5 to 6 tablespoons milk

In medium bowl, stir together powdered sugar and cocoa; set aside. In small mixer bowl, beat butter until creamy; add ½ cup powdered sugar mixture, corn syrup, if desired, and vanilla, beating until well blended. Add remaining powdered sugar mixture alternately with milk until of spreading consistency.

Yield: About 2 cups frosting.

CHOCOLATE FROSTING

2 bars (2 oz.) HERSHEY'S
Unsweetened Baking Chocolate
1 tablespoon butter

1 teaspoon vanilla extract
2 cups powdered sugar
⅓ cup milk

In small saucepan over very low heat, melt chocolate and butter. Remove from heat; cool to room temperature. Stir in vanilla. Add powdered sugar alternately with milk, beating until of spreading consistency.
Yield: About 1¾ cups frosting.

FLUFFY VANILLA ICING

1 cup (½ pt.) light cream
½ cup all-purpose flour
½ cup (1 stick) butter, softened

½ cup shortening
2 cups powdered sugar
1 teaspoon vanilla extract

In medium saucepan, stir light cream into flour. Cook over medium heat, stirring constantly, until smooth and very thick. Remove from heat. Place plastic wrap directly on surface.; refrigerate until cold. In large mixer bowl, beat butter and shortening until well blended. Gradually add powdered sugar and vanilla beating until blended. Add flour mixture; beat until light and fluffy.
Yield: About 3¾ cups frosting.

VANILLA DRIZZLE

1 cup powdered sugar

1 to 2 tablespoons hot water

In small bowl, stir together powdered sugar and enough water until mixture is smooth and of drizzling consistency.
Yield: About ½ cup.

SUGAR GLAZE

1½ cups powdered sugar   ½ teaspoon vanilla extract
2 to 3 tablespoons milk

In medium bowl, stir together powdered sugar, milk and vanilla extract.

CHOCOLATE GLAZE

1 bar (1 oz.) HERSHEY'S   ½ teaspoon butter
   Unsweetened Baking Chocolate

In top of double boiler over hot, not boiling, water melt chocolate and butter; stir until mixture is smooth. Cool slightly. Drizzle from tip of teaspoon around edge of frosted cake, allowing some to drizzle down sides or drizzle over top of vanilla icing for garnish.

TWO–TONE GLAZE

1½ cups powdered sugar   2 to 3 tablespoons plus 1 to 2
½ teaspoon vanilla extract   teaspoons, milk, divided
2 tablespoons HERSHEY'S Cocoa

In medium bowl, stir together powdered sugar, 2 to 3 tablespoons milk and vanilla extract. Pour half of mixture into small bowl; stir in cocoa and 1 to 2 teaspoons milk.

ALMOND BAR CHOCOLATE SAUCE

4 HERSHEY'S Milk Chocolate   ¼ cup milk
   Bars with Almonds (1.45 oz.
   each), broken into pieces

In heavy small saucepan, stir together chocolate bar pieces and milk. Cook over very low heat, stirring constantly, until chocolate is melted. Serve warm as a topping over cake, ice cream or other desserts.

Yield: About ¾ cup sauce.

COCOA CHOCOLATE SAUCE

¼ cup (½ stick) butter   2 tablespoons HERSHEY'S
2 bars (2 oz.) HERSHEY'S   Cocoa
   Unsweetened Baking Chocolate   ½ cup light cream
¾ cup sugar   1 teaspoon vanilla extract

In top of double boiler over hot, not boiling, water melt butter and baking chocolate. Stir in sugar and cocoa; cook 5 minutes, stirring occasionally. Stir in light cream and vanilla; cook, stirring constantly, until well blended. Serve warm sauce over ice cream, cake or other desserts.

Yield: About 1 cup sauce.

COCOA FUDGE SAUCE

¾ cup sugar   ½ cup milk
¼ cup HERSHEY'S Cocoa   ½ cup light corn syrup
1 tablespoon cornstarch   2 tablespoons butter
½ teaspoon salt   2 teaspoons vanilla extract

In small saucepan, stir together sugar, cocoa, cornstarch and salt. Add milk and corn syrup; stir to blend. Cook over medium heat, stirring constantly, until mixture boils; boil and stir 5 minutes. Remove from heat; stir in butter and vanilla. Cool, without stirring, until lukewarm. Serve as a topping for cake, ice cream or other desserts.

Yield: About 1¼ cups sauce.

CREAM CHEESE GLAZE

1½ ozs. (½ of 3 oz. pkg.)
   cream cheese, softened
¾ cup powdered sugar

2 to 3 teaspoons milk
½ teaspoon vanilla extract

In small bowl, beat cream cheese, powdered sugar, milk and vanilla extract until smooth.

CHOCOLATE HARD SAUCE

2 tablespoons butter, softened
3 tablespoons HERSHEY'S
   Syrup

⅔ cup powdered sugar
½ teaspoon vanilla extract
Dash salt

In small bowl, beat butter until creamy; gradually stir in syrup. Gradually add powdered sugar, vanilla and salt, beating until well blended. Refrigerate. Serve sauce over hot desserts.

Yield: About ½ cup sauce.

CHOCOLATE GELATIN SAUCE

1 teaspoon unflavored gelatin
2 tablespoons cold water
1 cup sugar
⅓ cup HERSHEY'S Cocoa

⅓ cup water
¼ teaspoon salt
1 teaspoon vanilla extract

In small cup, sprinkle gelatin over cold water; let stand 5 minutes. In small saucepan, stir together sugar, cocoa, ⅓ cup water and salt. Cook over medium heat, stirring constantly, until mixture boils. Boil and stir 3 minutes. Remove from heat. Add softened gelatin; stir until dissolved. Stir in vanilla. Serve warm or cold sauce over ice cream or other desserts.

Yield: About ¾ cup sauce.

COCOA MINT SAUCE

2 tablespoons butter
¼ cup HERSHEY'S Cocoa
½ cup sugar

⅓ cup light cream
¼ teaspoon vanilla extract
⅛ teaspoon mint extract

In small saucepan over low heat, melt butter; add cocoa. Cook, stirring constantly, until thickened. Add sugar and light cream; cook and stir until smooth. Remove from heat; stir in vanilla and mint extract. Cool slightly. Serve sauce, warm or at room temperature, over ice cream.

Yield: About ¾ cup sauce

CLEAR COCOA SAUCE

¾ cup sugar
¼ cup HERSHEY'S Cocoa
1 tablespoon cornstarch
Dash salt

1¼ cups hot water
1 tablespoon butter
1 teaspoon vanilla extract

In medium saucepan, stir together sugar, cocoa, cornstarch and salt; stir in water. Cook over medium heat, stirring constantly, until mixture boils and thickens slightly. Remove from heat; stir in butter and vanilla. Serve warm over ice cream or pudding.

Yield: About 1⅔ cups sauce.

CHOCOLATE CARAMEL SAUCE

¼ cup HERSHEY'S Syrup
2 tablespoons milk

1 tablespoon butter
12 light caramels, unwrapped

In small saucepan, combine syrup, milk, butter and caramels. Cook over low heat, stirring constantly, until mixture is smooth. Serve warm sauce over ice cream.

Yield: About ⅔ cup sauce.

SPECIAL HOME MADE PIES

American
Swiss Che
Cream Ch
Cream Cheese
Sliced or Fri
Egg Sala
Cream Che
Salami
Salami & B
Steak San

Ham or Bacon
and Eggs

Pies

CHOCOLATE CREAM PIE

9-inch baked pastry shell
2½ cups milk, divided
3 bars (3 oz.) HERSHEY'S
  Unsweetened Baking Chocolate
  broken into pieces
1 cup sugar

3 tablespoons all-purpose flour
3 tablespoons cornstarch
½ teaspoon salt
4 egg yolks, slightly beaten
2 tablespoons butter
1½ teaspoons vanilla extract

Prepare pastry shell; cool. In medium saucepan, combine 2 cups milk and chocolate. Cook over low heat, stirring occasionally, until chocolate is melted. In medium bowl, stir together flour, cornstarch, sugar and salt. Gradually add remaining ½ cup milk, stirring until smooth; stir into chocolate mixture. Cook over medium heat, stirring constantly, until mixture is thickened and bubbly. Remove from heat; gradually add about 1 cup hot mixture to egg yolks. Return all to saucepan; bring to gentle boil. Cook and stir 2 minutes. Remove from heat; stir in butter and vanilla. Pour into pastry shell. Press plastic wrap directly onto surface. Cool; refrigerate until firm. Garnish as desired.

Yield: 8 servings.

CHOCOLATE RAISIN PIE

1½ cups raisins
1 cup (½ pt.) light cream
⅓ cup HERSHEY'S Semi-Sweet
  Chocolate Chips
¼ cup (½ stick) butter
1 teaspoon vanilla extract
¾ cup sugar

3 tablespoons cornstarch
⅛ teaspoon ground cinnamon
⅛ teaspoon salt
2 eggs
9-inch unbaked pastry shell
Sweetened whipped cream
  (optional)

Heat oven to 375°F. In medium saucepan, stir together raisins, light cream, chocolate chips and butter. Cook over low heat, stirring constantly, until chips and butter are melted. Remove from heat; stir in vanilla. In medium bowl, stir together sugar, cornstarch, cinnamon and salt; stir into raisin mixture. In small bowl, beat eggs well; stir into raisin mixture. Pour into pastry shell. Bake 40 to 45 minutes or until filling is set. Cool. Top with whipped cream, if desired.

Yield: 8 servings.

COCOA CREAM PIE

8-inch baked pastry shell
¾ cup sugar
¼ cup HERSHEY'S Cocoa
3 tablespoons cornstarch
¼ teaspoon salt
2 cups milk

2 egg yolks, beaten
1 tablespoon butter
1 teaspoon vanilla extract
Sweetened whipped cream
Strawberries, halved (optional)

Prepare pastry shell; cool. In medium saucepan, stir together sugar, cocoa, cornstarch and salt. Gradually stir in milk. Cook over medium heat, stirring constantly, until mixture is thickened and bubbly. Boil 1 minute; remove from heat. Gradually stir about half of the hot filling into yolks. Return all to saucepan; bring to gentle boil. Cook and stir 1 minute. Remove from heat; stir in butter and vanilla. Pour into pastry shell. Press plastic wrap directly onto surface. Cool. Refrigerate until set. Garnish with whipped cream and strawberries, if desired.

Yield: 8 servings.

CHOCOLATE PIE

8-inch baked pastry shell
1 envelope unflavored gelatin
3 tablespoons cold water
1 cup HERSHEY'S Semi-Sweet
  Chocolate Chips
1¼ cups milk, divided
⅓ cup sugar

3 egg yolks, slightly beaten
½ teaspoon salt
1 teaspoon vanilla extract
1 cup (½ pt.) cold
  whipping cream
Sweetened whipped cream
Chopped walnuts

Prepare pastry shell; cool. In small bowl, sprinkle gelatin over water. Let stand 2 minutes to soften. In medium saucepan, combine chocolate chips and ½ cup milk; cook over low heat, stirring constantly, until chips are melted. Remove from heat. Add softened gelatin, remaining ¾ cup milk, sugar, egg yolks and salt. Cook over medium heat, stirring constantly, until mixture thickens. Remove from heat; stir in vanilla. Pour mixture into large bowl; press wax paper directly onto surface. Cool. Refrigerate until mixture mounds slightly when dropped from spoon. In small mixer bowl, beat 1 cup whipping cream until stiff; fold into chocolate mixture. Pour into pastry shell Refrigerate until set. Garnish with dollops of whipped cream and walnuts.

Yield: 8 servings.

CHOCOLATE BROWNIE PIE

3 bars (3 oz.) HERSHEY'S
  Unsweetened Baking Chocolate
3 eggs
1/3 cup butter, softened
1 1/2 cups sugar
3/4 cup all-purpose flour

1/2 teaspoon salt
1/3 cup milk
1 teaspoon vanilla extract
1 cup chopped nuts
Ice cream or whipped cream
(optional)

Heat oven to 375°F. Grease 9-inch pie plate. In top of double boiler over hot, not boiling, water melt chocolate; set aside to cool. In small bowl, beat eggs until very light; set aside. In small mixer bowl, beat butter until creamy; gradually add sugar, beating until light and fluffy. Add chocolate and eggs to butter mixture; beat until blended. Stir together flour and salt; add alternately with milk to butter mixture. Stir in vanilla and nuts. Pour mixture into prepared pie plate. Bake 40 to 45 minutes or until set. Cool. Serve with ice cream or whipped cream, if desired.

Yield: 8 servings.

CHOCOLATE BUTTERSCOTCH PIE

9-inch baked pastry shell
1 cup packed light brown sugar
1/3 cup cornstarch
1/2 teaspoon salt
4 egg yolks
3 cups milk

1 1/2 bars (1 1/2 oz.) HERSHEY'S
  Unsweetened Baking
  Chocolate, broken into pieces
1 tablespoon butter
1 teaspoon vanilla extract
Sweetened whipped cream

Prepare pastry shell; cool. In medium saucepan, stir together brown sugar, cornstarch and salt. Beat egg yolks with milk; gradually add to brown sugar mixture, stirring until well blended. Add chocolate. Cook over medium heat, stirring constantly, until mixture thickens and boils. Boil and stir 1 minute. Remove from heat; stir in butter and vanilla. Immediately pour mixture into pastry shell; press plastic wrap directly onto surface. Refrigerate 3 to 4 hours until filling is set. Garnish with whipped cream, if desired. Store, covered, in refrigerator.

Yield: 8 servings.

HOME FRONT COCONUT CREAM PIE

9-inch baked pastry shell
⅔ cup plus 9 tablespoons sugar, divided
⅓ cup cornstarch
¼ teaspoon salt
3 cups plus 2 tablespoons milk, divided
3 eggs, separated

1 tablespoon butter
2 teaspoons vanilla extract
½ cup flaked coconut
3 tablespoons HERSHEY'S Cocoa
¼ teaspoon cream of tartar
Additional flaked coconut (optional)

Prepare pastry shell; cool. In medium saucepan, stir together ⅔ cup sugar, cornstarch, salt and 3 cups milk; blend in beaten egg yolks. Cook over medium heat, stirring constantly, until mixture boils; boil and stir 1 minute. Remove from heat; stir in butter and vanilla. Into small bowl, pour 1½ cups cream filling; stir in coconut. Set aside. In separate bowl, stir together cocoa, 3 tablespoons sugar and remaining 2 tablespoons milk; stir into remaining cream filling in saucepan. Return to heat; cook, stirring constantly, just to boiling. Remove from heat; pour 1 cup chocolate filling into pastry shell. Spread coconut filling over chocolate layer. Top with remaining chocolate filling; spread evenly. Heat oven to 325°F. In small mixer bowl, beat egg whites with cream of tartar until foamy. Gradually add remaining 6 tablespoons sugar, beating until stiff peaks form. Spread meringue over hot pie filling, carefully sealing at edge of pastry. Bake 25 minutes; let cool 1 hour on wire rack. Sprinkle additional coconut over top, if desired. Refrigerate until cold.

Yield: 8 servings.

OUR GAL SUNDAE PIE

⅔ cup packed light brown sugar
3 tablespoons all-purpose flour
2 tablespoons cornstarch
½ teaspoon salt
½ cup (5.5-oz. can) HERSHEY'S
 Syrup
2¼ cups milk
3 egg yolks, well beaten
2 tablespoons butter
1 teaspoon vanilla extract
Maraschino cherries (optional)

Sweetened whipped cream
 (optional)
HERSHEY'S Milk Chocolate
 Bar, broken into squares
 (optional)
Macaroon Nut Crust:
 1¼ cups coconut macaroon
  cookie crumbs
 ½ cup chopped walnuts
 ¼ cup (½ stick) melted butter

Prepare Macaroon Nut Crust. In medium saucepan, stir together brown sugar, flour, cornstarch and salt. Gradually stir in milk, syrup and egg yolks. Cook over medium heat, stirring constantly, until mixture boils; boil and stir 1 minute. Remove from heat; stir in butter and vanilla. Pour into prepared crust; place plastic wrap directly on surface. Cool; refrigerate. Garnish with whipped cream, maraschino cherries and chocolate bar squares, if desired. Store, covered, in refrigerator.

Macaroon Nut Crust

Heat oven to 350°F. In medium bowl, stir together coconut macaroon cookie crumbs, chopped walnuts and melted butter. Press firmly onto bottom and up sides of 9-inch pie plate. Bake 8 to 10 minutes. Cool completely.

Yield: 8 servings.

Home Front Coconut Cream Pie

Desserts

Old-Fashioned Chocolate Ice Cream (page 58)

OLD-FASHIONED CHOCOLATE
ICE CREAM

3 envelopes unflavored gelatin
½ cup cold water
1 cup whole milk
¾ cup sugar
Dash salt

1½ cups (1-lb. can)
   HERSHEY'S Syrup
2 cups (1 pt.) light cream
2 cups (1 pt.) whipping cream
2 tablespoons vanilla extract

In medium saucepan, sprinkle gelatin over water; let stand 5 minutes. Add milk and sugar. Cook over low heat, stirring constantly, until gelatin is completely dissolved. Remove from heat; add salt and syrup, stirring until well blended. Cool. Refrigerate until cold. Stir together chocolate mixture, light cream, whipping cream and vanilla; pour into 5-quart ice cream freezer container. Freeze according to manufacturer's directions.

Yield: About 2 quarts ice cream.

CHOCOLATE ICE CREAM

2 bars (2 oz.) HERSHEY'S
   Unsweetened Baking Chocolate
1 can (14 oz.) sweetened
   condensed milk

1 cup water
1 cup (½ pt.) cold
   whipping cream
¼ teaspoon vanilla extract

In top of double boiler over hot, not boiling, water melt chocolate. Add sweetened condensed milk; continue to cook over hot water, stirring constantly, 5 minutes. Stir in water. Remove from heat; pour mixture into large bowl. Stir in vanilla. Cool. In small mixer bowl, beat whipping cream until stiff; gently fold into chocolate mixture until blended. Pour into 8-inch square pan. Cover; freeze 5 to 6 hours or until firm. Return leftovers to freezer.

Yield: 6 servings.

STEAMED CHOCOLATE PUDDING

2 bars (2 oz.) HERSHEY'S
   Unsweetened Baking Chocolate
¾ cup sugar
1 egg
½ teaspoon vanilla extract
1 cup all-purpose flour

1 tablespoon baking powder
¼ teaspoon salt
½ cup milk
2 tablespoons butter, melted
Chocolate Hard Sauce (page 46)

In top of double boiler over hot, not boiling, water melt chocolate. Set aside to cool slightly. In small mixer bowl, beat sugar, egg and vanilla until well blended. Stir together flour, baking powder and salt; add alternately with milk to sugar mixture, beating until well blended. Add butter and chocolate; beat until blended. Pour mixture into well-greased 4 or 5-cup mold; cover with foil. Place on a rack in a deep kettle; add boiling water to a depth of 1 inch. Cover kettle; boil gently 1½ hours. (Add more boiling water, if necessary, during cooking.) Remove mold from kettle. Cool 10 minutes; unmold onto serving dish. Serve warm with Chocolate Hard Sauce.

Yield: 12 servings.

COCOA MARBLE GINGERBREAD

½ cup shortening
1 cup sugar
1 cup light molasses
2 eggs
1 teaspoon baking soda
1 cup boiling water
2 cups all-purpose flour
1 teaspoon salt

¼ cup HERSHEY'S Cocoa
½ teaspoon ground cinnamon
½ teaspoon ground ginger
¼ teaspoon ground cloves
¼ teaspoon ground nutmeg
Sweetened whipped cream
  (optional)

Heat oven to 350°F. Grease and flour 13 x 9 x 2-inch baking pan. In large mixer bowl, beat shortening, sugar and molasses until blended; blend in eggs. Stir baking soda into boiling water to dissolve; add to shortening mixture alternately with combined flour and salt. Remove 2 cups batter to medium bowl; add cocoa, blending well. Add spice to remaining batter in large mixer bowl. Alternately spoon batters into prepared pan; with narrow spatula or knife swirl gently through batter to marble. Bake 40 to 45 minutes or until wooden pick inserted in center comes out clean. Cut into squares. Serve warm or cool with sweetened whipped cream, if desired.

Yield: About 12 servings.

CHOCOLATE BREAD PUDDING

4 cups French or Italian hard
   bread, torn into small pieces
   and lightly packed into
   measuring cup
1/4 cup (1/2 stick) butter,
   softened
1 1/4 cups sugar
3 cups (two 12-oz. cans)
   evaporated milk

3 eggs
1/4 cup HERSHEY'S Cocoa
2 teaspoons vanilla extract
1/2 teaspoon salt
1/4 teaspoon cream of tartar
1/2 cup golden raisins
1/2 cup chopped pecans
2 tablespoons coarsely chopped
   pecans (optional)

Heat oven to 400°F. Place bread in lightly buttered 2-quart casserole; set aside. In large mixer bowl, beat butter and sugar until well blended. Add evaporated milk, eggs, cocoa, vanilla, salt and cream of tartar; beat on low speed of mixer until blended. Stir in raisins and 1/2 cup pecans. Pour mixture over bread, making sure bread is covered with mixture. Sprinkle coarsely chopped pecans over top, if desired. Bake 45 to 50 minutes (place foil over top for last 10 minutes of baking) or until top is browned. Serve warm with light cream.

Yield: 8 servings.

CHOCOLATE BUTTERSCOTCH PUDDING

2/3 cup packed light brown sugar
1/3 cup all-purpose flour
1/2 teaspoon salt
2 cups (1 pt.) light cream
1/2 cup HERSHEY'S Syrup

2 egg yolks, slightly beaten
2 tablespoons butter
1/2 teaspoon vanilla extract
Sweetened whipped cream
   (optional)

In medium saucepan, stir together brown sugar, flour and salt. Gradually add light cream, stirring until well blended. Stir in syrup. Add egg yolks; stir until blended. Cook over medium heat, stirring constantly, until thickened. Remove from heat; stir in butter and vanilla. Pour into individual serving dishes. Cool; refrigerate until serving time. Serve with sweetened whipped cream, if desired.

Yield: 4 servings.

ORANGE CUSTARD–FILLED CHOCOLATE ROLL

3 eggs, separated
1 teaspoon vanilla extract
⅔ cup plus 1 tablespoon sugar, divided
½ cup all-purpose flour
⅓ cup HERSHEY'S Cocoa
½ teaspoon baking soda
¼ teaspoon salt
⅓ cup water
¾ cup cold whipping cream

2 tablespoons powdered sugar
Orange Custard Filling:
⅓ cup all-purpose flour
⅓ cup sugar
¼ teaspoon salt
1 cup milk
⅓ cup orange juice
2 egg yolks
¼ cup cold whipping cream

Prepare Orange Custard Filling. Heat oven to 375°F. Line 15½ x 10½ x 1-inch jelly roll pan with foil; generously grease foil. In large mixer bowl, beat egg yolks and vanilla on high speed of electric mixer about 3 minutes. Gradually add ⅓ cup sugar, beating until lemon colored. Stir together flour, cocoa, ⅓ cup sugar, baking soda and salt; add alternately with water to yolk mixture, beating on low speed just until batter is smooth. In small mixer bowl, beat egg whites until foamy; add remaining 1 tablespoon sugar, beating until stiff peaks form. Carefully fold beaten whites into chocolate mixture. Spread batter evenly into prepared pan. Bake 15 to 18 minutes or until top springs back when touched lightly in center. Immediately loosen cake from edges of pan; invert on towel sprinkled with powdered sugar. Carefully remove foil. Immediately roll cake in towel starting from narrow end; place on wire rack to cool. Unroll cake; remove towel. Spread with filling; reroll cake. Refrigerate until chilled. In small bowl, beat whipping cream and powdered sugar until stiff; spread over roll. Garnish as desired.

Orange Custard

In top of double boiler, stir together flour, sugar and salt. Gradually add milk, stirring until blended. Stir in orange juice. Cook over hot, not boiling, water, stirring constantly, until thickened, about 10 minutes. In small bowl, beat egg yolks; add about 1 cup hot mixture, stirring until blended. Return all of the egg mixture to top of double boiler. Cook, stirring constantly, until thickened, about 2 minutes. Remove from heat; pour into large bowl. Place wax paper directly on surface. Cool. Refrigerate until cold. In small mixer bowl, beat whipping cream until stiff; fold into custard mixture. *About 2 cups filling.*

Yield: 10 to 12 servings.

BAKED CHOCOLATE RICE PUDDING

½ cup regular long grain rice
1 cup water
⅔ cup plus ¼ cup sugar,
  divided
⅓ cup HERSHEY'S Cocoa

1 tablespoon cornstarch
Dash salt
2½ cups milk, divided
2 eggs, separated
½ cup raisins

In medium saucepan, stir together rice and water. Cook, stirring occasionally, to boiling; reduce heat. Cover and simmer 14 minutes without removing cover or stirring (all the water should be absorbed). Remove from heat; stir lightly with fork. Set aside. Heat oven to 350°F. In large bowl, stir together ⅔ cup sugar, cocoa, cornstarch and salt. Add ½ cup milk; stir until mixture is smooth. Gradually stir in remaining 2 cups milk. Add egg yolks; beat until well blended. Stir in rice and raisins. Place ungreased 1½-quart casserole in baking pan. Pour rice mixture into casserole. Pour hot water to 1-inch depth into baking pan around casserole. Bake, uncovered, about 1½ hours, stirring occasionally, until pudding is creamy and most of the liquid is absorbed. Remove casserole from oven, but not from baking pan. Increase oven temperature to 400°F. In small mixer bowl, beat egg whites until foamy. Gradually add remaining ¼ cup sugar, beating until stiff peaks form; spread over top of pudding. Return to oven. Bake 8 to 10 minutes or until lightly browned. Serve warm.

Yield: 12 servings.

COCOA CREAM TAPIOCA

2¾ cups milk
6 tablespoons HERSHEY'S Syrup
¼ cup quick-cooking tapioca
3 tablespoons sugar

¼ teaspoon salt
½ teaspoon vanilla extract
Sweetened whipped cream

In medium saucepan, bring milk to boil; stir in syrup, tapioca, sugar and salt. Cook over medium heat, stirring constantly, until thickened. Remove from heat; stir in vanilla. Cool, stirring occasionally, about 20 minutes or until bottom of saucepan is cool to the touch. Pour into individual serving dishes; press wax paper directly onto surface. Refrigerate. Garnish with whipped cream.

Yield: 5 servings.

CHOCOLATE BAVARIAN CREAM

1 envelope unflavored gelatin
¼ cup cold water
2 bars (2 oz.) HERSHEY'S
   Unsweetened Baking Chocolate
1 cup sugar
Dash salt
½ cup hot milk

1 teaspoon vanilla extract
2 cups (1 pt.) cold
   whipping cream
About 12 ladyfingers, split or
   24 strips sponge cake
Sweetened whipped cream
   (optional)

In small bowl, sprinkle gelatin over water; let stand 2 minutes. In top of double boiler over hot, not boiling, water melt chocolate. Add sugar, salt and milk; stir with whisk until well blended. Stir gelatin into hot mixture; stir until gelatin is completely dissolved. Remove from heat. Pour mixture into large bowl; cool 15 to 20 minutes. Beat until spongy and light, about 2 minutes; stir in vanilla. In large mixer bowl, beat whipping cream until stiff; fold into chocolate mixture. Line bottom and sides of 5- or 6- cup decorative mold with ladyfingers, cut side in. Pour chocolate mixture into mold. Cover with wax paper. Refrigerate until set, about 4 to 5 hours. Unmold onto serving plate. Garnish with sweetened whipped cream, if desired.
Yield: 12 servings.

CHOCOLATE MARSHMALLOW PUDDING

3 cups milk
½ cup (5½ oz. can)
   HERSHEY'S Syrup
¼ cup sugar
3 tablespoons all-purpose flour

Dash salt
1 egg
1 teaspoon vanilla extract
1 cup minature marshmallows

Heat oven to 400°F. In medium saucepan, stir milk and syrup. Cook over medium heat until tiny bubbles form at edges of pan. In medium bowl, stir together sugar, flour, salt and egg. Stir about half of the hot milk mixture into sugar mixture. Return all to saucepan; cook, stirring constantly, until mixture just begins to boil. Reduce heat; cook and stir 2 minutes. Remove from heat; stir in vanilla. Pour mixture into 1½ quart baking dish; top with marshmallows. Place in oven until marshmallows are lightly browned, about 5 minutes. Cool; refrigerate. Serve cold.
Yield: 12 servings.

COCOA MERINGUE CAKE

½ cup (1 stick) butter, softened
⅔ cup plus ½ cup sugar,
  divided
4 eggs, separated
1 cup all-purpose flour
¼ cup HERSHEY'S Cocoa

1½ teaspoons baking powder
¼ teaspoon cream of tartar
½ cup milk
½ teaspoon vanilla extract
¼ cup chopped pecans
Cocoa Cream Filling (page 39)

Heat oven to 325°F. Grease and flour two 9-inch round baking pans. In large mixer bowl, beat butter and ⅔ cup sugar until light and fluffy. Add egg yolks; beat well. Stir together flour, cocoa and baking powder; add alternately with milk to butter mixture, beating until well blended. Spread batter into prepared pans. In small mixer bowl, beat egg whites and cream of tartar until foamy. Gradually add remaining ½ cup sugar and vanilla, beating until stiff peaks form. Carefully spread egg white mixture over cake batter in pans. Sprinkle pecans on top. Bake 25 to 30 minutes or until meringue is golden. Cool 10 minutes. Loosen edges; gently invert onto wire racks. Remove pans. Place a second wire rack on cake bottoms; invert again so meringue sides are up. Cool completely. Place one cake layer on serving plate, meringue side up. Spread Cocoa Cream Filling on top of meringue. Top with remaining cake layer, meringue side up.

Yield: 8 servings.

MOCHA CHOCOLATE MARLOW

1½ squares (1½ oz.)
  HERSHEY'S Unsweetened
  Baking Chocolate
½ cup strong coffee
1 cup marshmallow creme

¼ cup sugar
Dash salt
1 cup (½ pt.) cold
  whipping cream
⅓ cup chopped nuts

In medium saucepan, combine baking chocolate and coffee. Cook over low heat, stirring constantly, until chocolate is melted. Remove from heat; add marshmallow cream, sugar and salt, stirring until blended. Cool; refrigerate until mixture is cold and slightly thickened. In small mixer bowl, beat whipping cream until stiff; fold whipped cream and nuts into chocolate mixture. Pour into 8-inch square pan. Cover; freeze until firm, about 6 hours.

Yield: 8 servings.

CHOCOLATE CUSTARD ICE CREAM

2 cups sugar
¼ cup all-purpose flour
⅛ teaspoon salt
2 cups whole milk
2 eggs, slightly beaten

4 bars (4 oz.) HERSHEY'S
   Unsweetened Baking
   Chocolate, broken into pieces
4 cups (2 pt.) light cream
2 tablespoons vanilla extract

In medium saucepan, stir together sugar, flour and salt. Gradually stir in milk. Add eggs and chocolate pieces. Cook over medium heat, stirring constantly, until mixture thickens and begins to boil; boil and stir 1 minute. Cool; refrigerate until cold. Stir together chocolate mixture, light cream and vanilla. Fill ice cream freezer container no more than ⅔ full. Freeze according to manufacturer's directions.

Yield: About 2 quarts ice cream.

QUICK CREAMY CHOCOLATE PUDDING

⅔ cup sugar
¼ cup HERSHEY'S Cocoa
3 tablespoons cornstarch
¼ teaspoon salt
2¼ cups milk

2 tablespoons butter
1 teaspoon vanilla extract
Sweetened whipped cream
  (optional)
Chopped nuts (optional)

In medium saucepan, stir together sugar, cocoa, cornstarch and salt; gradually stir in milk. Cook over medium heat, stirring constantly, until mixture boils; boil and stir 1 minute. Remove from heat; stir in butter and vanilla. Pour into individual serving dishes. Press wax paper directly onto surface. Refrigerate . Garnish with whipped cream and nuts, if desired.

Yield: 4 to 5 servings.

FIRESIDE STEAMED PUDDING

1½ cups plain dry bread
crumbs
1 cup sugar, divided
2 tablespoons all-purpose flour
½ teaspoon baking powder
⅛ teaspoon salt
6 eggs, separated
1 can (21 oz.) cherry pie filling,
divided
½ teaspoon almond extract

2 tablespoons butter, melted
¼ teaspoon red food color
1 cup HERSHEY'S Mini
Chips Semi-Sweet Chocolate
Cherry Whipped Cream:
1 cup (½ pt.) cold whipping
cream
¼ cup powdered sugar
½ teaspoon almond extract

Thoroughly grease 8-cup tube mold or heat-proof bowl. In large bowl, stir together bread crumbs, ¾ cup sugar, flour, baking powder and salt. In medium bowl, stir together egg yolks, 1½ cups cherry pie filling, butter, almond extract and food color; add to crumb mixture, stirring gently until well blended. In large mixer bowl, beat egg whites until foamy; gradually add remaining ¼ cup sugar, beating until stiff peaks form. Fold about one-third beaten whites into cherry mixture, blending thoroughly. Fold in remaining egg whites; gently fold in small chocolate chips. Pour batter into prepared tube mold. (If mold is open at top, cover opening with foil; grease top of foil.) Cover mold with wax paper and foil; tie securely with string. Place a rack in a large kettle; pour water into kettle to top of rack. Bring water to boil; place mold on rack. Cover kettle; steam over simmering water about 1½ hours or until wooden pick inserted comes out clean. (Additional water may be needed during steaming.) Remove from heat; cool in pan 5 minutes. Remove cover; unmold onto serving plate. Serve warm with Cherry Whipped Cream.

Cherry Whipped Cream

In small mixer bowl, beat cream with powdered sugar until stiff; fold in pie filling remaining from pudding (about ½ cup) and almond extract.

Yield: 12 to 14 servings.

Quick Creamy Chocolate Pudding (page 69) Chocolate Souffle (page 73)
Fireside Steamed Pudding;,Chocolate Cream Eclairs (page 72)

CHOCOLATE CREAM ECLAIRS

½ cup (1 stick) butter
1 cup water
¼ teaspoon salt
1 cup all-purpose flour
4 eggs
Chocolate Cream Filling:
   5 tablespoons cornstarch
   ¼ cup sugar
   ¼ teaspoon salt

3 cups milk
3 egg yolks, slightly beaten
1 teaspoon vanilla extract
1 HERSHEY'S Milk Chocolate
   Bar (7 oz.), broken into pieces
Eclair Glaze:
   1 HERSHEY'S Milk Chocolate
   Bar (4 oz.), broken into pieces
   4 teaspoons water

Prepare Chocolate Cream Filling. Heat oven to 400°F. Grease cookie sheet. In medium saucepan, combine butter, water and salt. Cook over medium heat to rolling boil, stirring until butter melts. Add flour all at once; reduce heat. Stir vigorously over low heat until mixture forms a ball that does not separate. Remove from heat; cool 10 minutes. Add eggs, one at a time, beating with spoon after each addition about 1 minute or until smooth. On prepared cookie sheet, shape scant ¼ cup dough into fingers 4 inches long and 1 inch wide, 3 inches apart. Bake 35 to 40 minutes or until puffed and golden brown. Remove eclairs from cookie sheet to wire rack; cool. To assemble, horizontally slice off small portion from top of each eclair; set aside. Remove any soft dough from inside. Spoon about ¼ cup filling into each eclair; replace tops. Spread Eclair Glaze over tops. Refrigerate until serving time. Refrigerate any remaining eclairs.

Chocolate Cream Filling

In medium saucepan, stir together cornstarch, sugar and salt. Gradually add milk, stirring until blended. Stir in egg yolks. Cook over medium heat, stirring constantly, until mixture boils; boil and stir 1 minute. Remove from heat; add vanilla and chocolate bar pieces, stirring until chocolate is melted. Pour into large bowl; press wax paper directly onto surface. Cool. *About 4 cups filling.*

Eclair Glaze

In top of double boiler over hot, not boiling, water melt chocolate bar pieces with water; stir to blend. (An additional teaspoon water may be added if glaze is too thick.) If chocolate thickens or becomes grainy, add shortening, 1 teaspoon at a time, stirring until mixture becomes smooth. *About ⅓ cup glaze.*

Yield: 12 eclairs.

Friends Shop Contact Numbers
Updated June 2014

*Mary Griffard   (Shop Manager)   734-482-2418
Jaci Faul   (Volunteer Coordinator) 734-434-9437

Shop Substitutes

Lynn Allen	484-0551
Madeline Balogh	485-6815
Mary Bowman	461-6781
*Mary Woods	483=1034
Jade Henopp	657-2665

Substitutes– If you are unable to work your scheduled shift, please call Lynn Allen, Madeline Balogh, Mary Bowman, Mary Woods or Jade Henopp who have graciously volunteered to be shop substitutes.

If they are not available, call Volunteer Coordinator Jaci or Shop Manager Mary. Copies of all our contact numbers are located in the Shop Manual.

Leaving a message at the shop number should be your last resort, since often no one is there to take the message.

Thanks for all you do for the Friends Shop,
Mary and Jaci

* This indicates change from previous lists.

CHOCOLATE SOUFFLE

2 envelopes unflavored gelatin
²⁄₃ cup sugar
¹⁄₃ cup HERSHEY'S Cocoa
2¹⁄₄ cups milk

3 egg yolks, beaten
³⁄₄ teaspoon vanilla extract
1¹⁄₂ cups cold whipping cream

Measure length of aluminum foil to fit around 1-quart souffle dish; fold in thirds lengthwise. Lightly oil one side of collar; tape securely to outside of dish, oiled side in, allowing collar to extend 3 inches above rim of dish. Set aside. In medium saucepan, stir together gelatin, sugar and cocoa; stir in milk and egg yolks. Let stand 2 minutes. Cook over low heat, stirring constantly, until gelatin is completely dissolved. Remove from heat; stir in vanilla. Pour mixture into large bowl; refrigerate, stirring occasionally, until mixture mounds slightly when dropped from spoon. In small mixer bowl, beat whipping cream until stiff; fold into chocolate mixture. Pour into prepared dish; refrigerate 4 to 6 hours or until set. Just before serving, carefully remove foil. Garnish as desired.

Yield: 6 to 8 servings.

Breads

Chocolate Tea Bread (page 82),
Chocolate Dessert Waffles (page 76)

NOSTALGIA DATE–NUT LOAVES

1½ cups boiling water
1 cup dates, chopped
1¼ cups sugar
1 egg
1 tablespoon vegetable oil
2 teaspoons vanilla extract
2 cups all-purpose flour

2 teaspoons baking soda
½ teaspoon salt
¼ teaspoon baking powder
1 cup chopped walnuts
1 cup HERSHEY'S MINI CHIPS
   Semi-Sweet Chocolate
Walnut halves (optional)

In bowl, pour water over dates; let stand 15 minutes. Heat oven to 350°F. Grease four 3¼ x 5¾ x 2¼-inch small loaf pans. In large mixer bowl, beat sugar and egg on high speed of electric mixer 3 minutes. Add oil and vanilla; beat until well blended. Stir together flour, baking soda, salt and baking powder; add alternately with dates to egg mixture, beating until blended. Stir in chopped walnuts and small chocolate chips. Pour about 1¼ cups batter into each prepared pan. Bake 40 to 50 minutes or until wooden pick inserted in center comes out clean. Cool 10 minutes; remove from pans to wire racks. Cool completely. Garnish with walnut halves, if desired.

Yield: 4 loaves.

CHOCOLATE DESSERT WAFFLES

½ cup (1 stick) butter
2 bars (2 oz.) HERSHEY'S
   Unsweetened Baking Chocolate
¾ cup sugar
1 teaspoon vanilla extract
2 eggs

1½ cups all-purpose flour
1 teaspoon cream of tartar
½ teaspoon baking soda
½ cup buttermilk
1 cup chopped nuts
Vanilla ice cream

In medium saucepan over low heat, melt butter and chocolate. Add sugar and vanilla; stir until blended. Remove from heat; add eggs, one at a time, beating after each addition until well blended. Stir together flour, cream of tartar and baking soda; add alternately with buttermilk to chocolate mixture. Stir in nuts. Bake in waffle iron according to manufacturer's directions. Carefully remove waffle from iron. (When first taken from waffle iron, the waffle will be soft, but will become crisp as it cools.) Serve warm with scoop of ice cream.

Yield: About twelve 5-inch waffles.

CHOCOLATE–PECAN FILLED BRAID

2½ to 2¾ cups all-purpose flour,
 divided
2 tablespoons sugar
½ teaspoon salt
1 package active dry yeast
½ cup milk
¼ cup water
½ cup butter
1 egg

Vanilla Drizzle (page 42)
Chocolate Pecan Filling:
 2 egg whites
 ⅓ cup sugar
 2 cups ground pecans
 1 cup HERSHEY'S MINI
  CHIPS Semi-Sweet Chocolate
 Dash ground cinnamon

Grease cookie sheet; set aside. In large mixer bowl, stir together 1 cup flour, sugar, salt and yeast. In small saucepan combine milk, water and butter; cook over low heat until liquids are very warm (120°F. to 130°F). (Butter does not need to melt.) Gradually add milk mixture to flour mixture, beating on medium speed of electric mixer 2 minutes. Add egg and ½ cup flour; beat on high speed 2 minutes. Stir in enough of the remaining flour to make a stiff dough. Cover bowl with plastic wrap and towel; set aside 20 minutes. Divide dough in half. Turn one part onto heavily floured surface; roll into 13 x 8-inch rectangle. Spread half of Chocolate Pecan Filling (about 1½ cups) lengthwise down center third of dough. Cut 1-inch wide strips diagonally along both sides of filling to within ¾-inch of filling Alternately fold opposite strips of dough at an angle across filling. Carefully transfer to prepared cookie sheet; pinch ends together. Repeat with remaining dough. Cover loosely with wax paper that has been brushed with vegetable oil, oiled side down. Top with plastic wrap. Refrigerate 2 to 24 hours. Remove from refrigerator 10 minutes before baking. Heat oven to 375°F. Uncover dough carefully; let stand at room temperature 10 minutes. Bake 30 to 35 minutes or until lightly browned. Remove from cookie sheet to wire rack; brush with butter. Cool completely. Drizzle Vanilla Drizzle over top.

Chocolate Pecan Filling

In small mixer bowl, beat egg whites until foamy. Gradually add sugar, beating until stiff peaks form. Fold in pecans, small chocolate chips and cinnamon. About 3 cups filling.

Yield: 2 braids.

SPICED COCOA DOUGHNUTS

2¼ cups all-purpose flour
½ cup HERSHEY'S Cocoa
2½ teaspoons baking powder
½ teaspoon baking soda
¼ teaspoon ground cinnamon
¼ teaspoon ground mace
¼ teaspoon salt

1½ tablespoons butter, softened
¾ cup granulated sugar
1 egg
½ cup milk
¼ cup powdered sugar
Dash ground cinnamon

In medium bowl, stir together flour, cocoa, baking powder, baking soda, ¼ teaspoon cinnamon, mace and salt. In large bowl, beat butter and sugar until creamy. Add egg; beat well. Add flour mixture alternately with milk, mixing until well blended; shape into ball. On lightly floured surface, roll dough to ¼ inch thickness. With floured 2½-inch doughnut cutter, cut into rings. Reroll dough as necessary. Fry two or three doughnuts at a time in deep hot fat (375°F) about 30 seconds, turning once with slotted spoon. Drain on paper towels. Repeat with remaining doughnuts. Stir together powdered sugar and dash cinnamon; sprinkle over top of warm doughnuts.

Yield: About 2 dozen doughnuts.

BRIDGE PARTY COFFEE CAKE

1 cup (2 sticks) butter, softened
2¼ cups sugar, divided
2 eggs
1 cup dairy sour cream
1 teaspoon freshly grated
 lemon peel
1 teaspoon lemon juice
2 cups all-purpose flour

1 teaspoon baking powder
¼ teaspoon salt
1 cup chopped nuts
½ cup shredded coconut
¼ cup HERSHEY'S Cocoa
1 teaspoon ground cinnamon
2 tablespoons butter, melted

Heat oven to 350°F. Grease and flour 12-cup fluted tube pan or 10-inch tube pan. In large mixer bowl, beat 1 cup butter, 2 cups sugar and eggs until light and fluffy. Add sour cream, lemon peel and juice; beat well. Stir together flour, baking powder and salt; add to butter mixture, beating well. In small bowl, stir together nuts, coconut, cocoa, remaining ¼ cup sugar, and cinnamon; sitr in melted butter. Spoon half of batter into prepared pan. Sprinkle half of nut mixture over batter. Top with remaining batter. Sprinkle remaining nut mixture over top. Bake 1 hour and 5 to 10 minutes or until wooden pick inserted comes out clean. Cool 10 minutes; remove from pan to wire rack. Cool completely. Sprinkle powdered sugar over top, if desired.

Yield: 12 to 14 servings.

MINI CHIP HARVEST RING

¾ cup all-purpose flour
¾ cup whole wheat flour*
¾ cup granulated sugar
½ cup packed light brown sugar
2 teaspoons ground cinnamon
1¼ teaspoons baking soda
½ teaspoon salt
3 eggs

¾ cup vegetable oil
1½ teaspoons vanilla extract
2 cups grated carrot, apple or
  zucchini, drained
¾ cup HERSHEY'S MINI
  CHIPS Semi-Sweet Chocolate
½ cup chopped walnuts
Cream Cheese Glaze (page 46)

Heat oven to 350°F. Grease and flour 6- or 8- cup fluted tube pan. In large bowl, stir together all-purpose flour, whole wheat flour, granulated sugar, brown sugar, cinnamon, baking soda and salt. In small bowl, beat eggs, oil and vanilla; add to flour mixture. With spoon, stir mixture until well blended. Stir in carrot, small chocolate chips and walnuts. Pour batter into prepared pan. Bake 45 to 50 minutes or until wooden pick inserted in center comes out clean. Cool 30 minutes; remove from pan to serving plate. Drizzle Cream Cheese Glaze over top and sides.

Yield: 8 to 10 servings

*All-purpose flour may be substituted for whole wheat flour.

ORANGE–COCOA AFTERNOON BISCUITS

1¾ cups all-purpose flour
½ cup HERSHEY'S Cocoa
½ cup sugar
4 teaspoons baking powder
½ teaspoon salt

3 tablespoons butter
¾ cup milk
¼ cup orange juice
24 sugar cubes

Heat oven to 425°F. Paper-line 24 muffin cups (2½ inches in diameter). In large bowl, stir together flour, cocoa, sugar, baking powder and salt. With knife or pastry blender, cut in butter; gradually add milk, stirring until blended. On lightly floured surface, roll dough to ¼-inch thickness. With floured cutter, cut into 2½-inch rounds; place in prepared cups. Place sugar cubes in orange juice; let stand 5 minutes. Place one cube in center of each round. Bake 14 to 16 minutes or until outer edges are puffed and firm. Serve hot.

Yield: 2 dozen biscuits.

CHOCOLATE CHIP ORANGE MUFFINS

1 egg
½ cup milk
¼ cup vegetable oil
1½ cups all-purpose flour
½ cup sugar
2 teaspoons baking powder

½ teaspoon salt
¾ cup HERSHEY'S Milk
   Chocolate Chips
1 to 1½ teaspoons freshly grated
   orange peel

Heat oven to 400°F. Grease 12 muffin cups (2½ inches in diameter). In medium bowl, beat egg; stir in milk and oil. Stir together flour, sugar, baking powder and salt; add all at once to egg mixture. Stir just until moistened (batter should be lumpy). Stir in chocolate chips and orange peel. Fill prepared muffin cups ⅔ full with batter. Bake 20 to 25 minutes or until lightly browned. Remove from pans; serve warm.

Yield: 12 muffins.

BERRY LOAF

2 cups all-purpose flour
1 cup sugar
1½ teaspoons baking powder
1 teaspoon salt
½ teaspoon baking soda
¾ cup orange juice
2 tablespoons shortening
1 egg, slightly beaten
1 teaspoon grated orange peel

1 cup chopped fresh cranberries
1 cup HERSHEY'S MINI CHIPS
   Semi-Sweet Chocolate
¾ cup chopped nuts
Glaze:
   1 cup powdered sugar
   1 tablespoon milk
   1 teaspoon butter, softened
   ½ teaspoon vanilla extract

Heat oven to 350°F. Grease 9 x 5 x 3-inch loaf pan. In large bowl, stir together flour, sugar, baking powder, salt and baking soda. Add orange juice, shortening, egg and orange peel; with spoon, stir until well blended. Stir in cranberries, small chocolate chips and nuts. Pour batter into prepared pan. Bake 1 hour and 5 to 10 minutes or until wooden pick inserted in center comes out clean. Cool 10 minutes; remove from pan. Spread Glaze over top of loaf, if desired. Cool completely. Garnish as desired.

Glaze

In small bowl, stir together powdered sugar, milk, butter and vanilla extract; beat until smooth. (If thinner glaze is desired, add milk, 1 teaspoon at a time.)

Yield: 1 loaf.

Chocolate Chip Orange Muffins; Chocolate-Pecan Filled Braid (page 77)

81

CHOCOLATE TEA BREAD

¼ cup (½ stick) butter, softened
⅔ cup sugar
1 egg
1½ cups all-purpose flour
⅓ cup HERSHEY'S Cocoa
1 teaspoon baking soda

¼ teaspoon salt
1 cup buttermilk
½ cup dairy sour cream
¾ cup chopped nuts
¾ cup raisins

Heat oven to 350°F. Grease 8 x 4 x 2-inch loaf pan. In large mixer bowl, beat butter until creamy. Gradually add sugar, beating until well blended. Add egg; beat well. Stir together flour, cocoa, baking soda and salt; add alternately with buttermilk to butter mixture. Stir in sour cream. Add nuts and raisins; stir until blended. Pour batter into prepared pan. Bake 1 hour and 15 to 20 minutes or until wooden pick inserted in center comes out clean. Cool 10 minutes; remove from pan to wire rack. Cool completely. Serve with softened cream cheese, if desired.

Yield: 1 loaf.

RAISIN–NUT COCOA BREAD

2 packages active dry yeast
½ cup warm water (110°F
  to 115°F)
2 cups cooked oatmeal, lukewarm
1 cup packed light brown sugar
2 tablespoons butter, softened

1 cup chopped nuts
1 cup chopped raisins or dates
½ teaspoon salt
6 to 6½ cups all-purpose flour,
  divided
½ cup HERSHEY'S Cocoa

Grease two 9 x 5 x 3-inch loaf pans. In small bowl, soften yeast in water. In large bowl, stir together brown sugar, butter, nuts, raisins and salt; add oatmeal and yeast mixture, stirring to blend. Stir together 2 cups flour and cocoa; add to cereal mixture, beat until well blended. Stir in as much of the remaining flour as you can mix in with a spoon. Turn out onto lightly floured surface. Knead in enough of the remaining flour to make a stiff dough that is smooth and elastic. Shape into a ball. Place in lightly greased bowl; turn over to grease top. Cover; let rise in warm place until double. Punch down dough; divide in half. Cover; let rest 10 minutes. Shape each half of dough into a loaf; place in prepared pans. Cover; let rise in warm place until almost double. Heat oven to 375°F. Bake loaves 30 to 35 minutes (if necessary, cover loosely with foil the last 15 minutes of baking to prevent overbrowning). Remove bread to wire racks. Brush tops of warm loaves with butter.

Yield: 2 loaves.

WALNUT KUCHEN

2½ to 2¾ cups all-purpose flour, divided
¼ cup sugar
½ teaspoon salt
1 package active dry yeast
½ cup dairy sour cream
¼ cup water
2 tablespoons milk
2 egg yolks (reserve whites for filling)
¼ cup (½ stick) butter

Walnut-Chip Filling:
2 egg whites
⅓ cup sugar
Dash salt
2 cups ground walnuts
1 cup HERSHEY'S MINI CHIPS Semi-Sweet Chocolate

Sugar Glaze or Two-Tone Glaze (optional, page 43)

Grease cookie sheet; set aside. In large mixer bowl, stir together 1 cup flour, sugar, salt and yeast; set aside. In small saucepan, stir together sour cream, butter, water and milk. Cook over low heat, stirring occasionally, until very warm (120°F to 130°F). Gradually add to flour mixture; beat on medium speed of electric mixer 2 minutes. Add egg yolks and ½ cup flour; beat on high speed 2 minutes. Gradually stir in enough flour to make a soft dough. When dough becomes difficult to stir, turn out onto well-floured surface. Knead in enough remaining flour until dough is elastic and forms smooth ball, 3 to 5 minutes. Cover; allow to rest 15 minutes. Divide dough in half. On lightly floured surface, roll each half into 12 x 10-inch rectangle Spread about 1¼ cups filling onto each rectangle to within ½ inch of edges. Roll up, jelly roll style, starting from one of the long sides; pinch to seal edges. Place on prepared cookie sheet, sealed edge up, just slightly curving roll. Cover with towel; let rise in warm place until doubled, about 1 to 1½ hours. Heat oven to 350°F. Bake 20 minutes. Loosely cover with foil; bake additional 15 minutes or until golden brown. Remove from cookie sheet to wire rack; brush lightly with butter. Cool completely. Just before serving, drizzle Sugar Glaze or Two-Tone Glaze over top.

Walnut-Chip Filling

In small mixer bowl, beat egg whites until foamy. Gradually add sugar and salt, beating until stiff peaks form. Fold in walnuts and small chocolate chips. *About 2½ cups filling.*

Yield: 2 loaves.

Cookies

Chocolatetown Chip Cookies (page 86)

CHOCOLATETOWN CHIP COOKIES

¾ cup (1½ sticks) butter,
softened
1 cup packed light brown sugar
½ cup granulated sugar
1 teaspoon vanilla extract
2 eggs

2 cups all-purpose flour
1 teaspoon baking soda
1 teaspoon salt
2 cups (12-oz. pkg.)
HERSHEY'S Semi-Sweet
Chocolate Chips

Heat oven to 375°F. In large mixer bowl, beat butter, brown sugar, granulated sugar and vanilla until light and fluffy. Add eggs; beat well. Stir together flour, baking soda and salt; gradually add to butter mixture, beating until blended. Stir in chocolate chips. Drop by teaspoonfuls onto ungreased cookie sheet. Bake 8 to 10 minutes or until lightly browned. Remove from cookie sheet to wire rack. Cool completely.

Yield: About 6 dozen cookies.

CAROL'S CHOCOLATE COCONUT SQUARES

⅓ cup butter, softened
1½ cups packed light
brown sugar
2 eggs
1 teaspoon vanilla extract
1 cup all-purpose flour
¼ cup HERSHEY'S Cocoa
1¼ teaspoons baking powder

½ teaspoon salt
½ cup milk
½ cup graham cracker crumbs,
rolled fine
¾ cup finely chopped walnuts
½ cup shredded coconut
Powdered sugar (optional)

Heat oven to 375°F. Grease 13 x 9 x 2-inch baking pan. In large mixer bowl, beat butter until creamy. Add brown sugar; beat well. Add eggs and vanilla; beat well. Stir together flour, cocoa, baking powder and salt; add alternately with milk to butter mixture. Add graham cracker crumbs; beat well. Stir in walnuts and coconut. Spread batter into prepared pan. Bake 25 minutes or until edges are set. Cool in pan on wire rack. Sprinkle powdered sugar over top, if desired. Cut into squares.

Yield: About 3 dozen squares.

CHOCOLATE COCONUT MACAROONS

2 bars (2 oz.) HERSHEY'S
  Unsweetened Baking Chocolate
3 cups shredded coconut

1 can (14 oz.) sweetened
  condensed milk
1 teaspoon vanilla extract

Heat oven to 350°F. Generously grease cookie sheet. In top of double boiler over hot, not boiling, water melt chocolate. In large bowl, stir together chocolate and sweetened condensed milk. Add coconut and vanilla; stir until well blended. Drop by teaspoonfuls onto prepared cookie sheet. Bake 15 minutes or until set. Do not overbake. Immediately remove from cookie sheet to wire rack. (Macaroons will stick if allowed to cool on cookie sheet.) Cool completely.

Yield: About 2½ dozen cookies.

CHOCOLATE OATMEAL RAISIN COOKIES

1 cup shortening
1⅓ cups sugar
2 eggs
2 cups all-purpose flour
⅓ cup HERSHEY'S Cocoa
1 teaspoon baking soda

1 teaspoon salt
1 teaspoon ground cinnamon
½ cup milk
2 cups quick-cooking rolled oats
1 cup raisins
1 cup chopped nuts (optional)

Heat oven to 350°F. Lightly grease cookie sheet. In large mixer bowl, beat shortening and sugar until creamy. Add eggs; blend well. Stir together flour, cocoa, baking soda, salt and cinnamon; add alternately with milk to shortening mixture beating well after each addition. Gradually stir in oats, raisins and nuts, if desired. Drop by teaspoonfuls onto prepared cookie sheet. Bake 10 to 12 minutes. Cool 1 minute; remove from cookie sheet to wire rack. Cool completely.

Yield: About 5 dozen cookies.

CHOCOLATE ROBINS

2 bars (2 oz.) HERSHEY'S
   Unsweetened Baking Chocolate
1/2 cup (1 stick) butter
3 eggs
1 cup sugar
3/4 cup all-purpose flour

1/2 teaspoon baking powder
1/2 teaspoon salt
Dash ground cinnamon
3/4 cup chopped nuts
1/4 cup chopped dates or raisins

Heat oven to 350°F. Grease 9-inch square baking pan. In small saucepan over low heat, melt chocolate and butter; set aside to cool slightly. In small mixer bowl, beat eggs and sugar until well blended. Add chocolate mixture; beat well. Stir together flour, baking powder, salt and cinnamon; add to butter mixture, beating until well blended. Stir in nuts and dates. Spread batter into prepared pan. Bake 25 minutes or until edges are set. Cool in pan on wire rack. Cut into squares.
Yield: 16 squares.

CHOCOLATE PINKS

3 tablespoons butter, softened
1/2 cup sugar
1 egg, separated
1/2 teaspoon vanilla extract
2/3 cup all-purpose flour
3 tablespoons HERSHEY'S
   Cocoa

1/4 teaspoon baking soda
1/2 cup milk
Pink Butter Icing (page 37)
2 HERSHEY'S Milk Chocolate
   Bars with Almonds
   (1.45 oz. each)

Heat oven to 350°F. Butter miniature muffin cups (1 3/4 inches in diameter). In small mixer bowl, beat butter and sugar until light and fluffy. Add egg yolk and vanilla; beat well. Stir together flour, cocoa and baking soda; add alternately with milk to butter mixture. Beat egg white until stiff peaks form; fold into batter. Fill prepared muffin cups one-half full with batter. Bake 13 to 15 minutes or until wooden pick inserted in center comes out clean. Cool 5 minutes; remove from cups to wire rack. Cool completely. Frost with Pink Butter Icing. Cut chocolate bars into small pieces; place on top of each cupcake while icing is still soft.
Yield: About 2 dozen small cupcakes.

Chocolate Robins, Chocolate Pinks;
Chocolate Midgets (page 90)

CHOCOLATE SYRUP BROWNIES

1 egg
1 cup packed light brown sugar
¾ cup HERSHEY'S Syrup
1½ cups all-purpose flour

¼ teaspoon baking soda
Dash salt
½ cup (1 stick) butter, melted
¾ cup chopped pecans or walnuts

Heat oven to 350°F. Grease 9-inch square baking pan. In small mixer bowl beat egg; add brown sugar and syrup, beating until well blended. Stir together flour, baking soda and salt; add to egg mixture, beating until blended. Fold in butter and nuts. Spread batter into prepared pan. Bake 35 to 40 minutes or until brownies begin to pull away from sides of pan. Cool in pan on wire rack. Cut into squares.

Yield: 16 brownies.

CHOCOLATE MIDGETS

½ cup (1 stick) butter
½ cup (5½-oz. can)
   HERSHEY'S Syrup
2 eggs
¾ cup sugar

1 teaspoon vanilla extract
¾ cup all-purpose flour
¼ teaspoon baking powder
1 cup chopped nuts

Heat oven to 350°F. Grease and flour 9-inch square baking pan. In small saucepan over low heat, melt butter; stir in syrup. Remove from heat; set aside to cool slightly. In small mixer bowl, beat eggs; add sugar and vanilla, beating until well blended. Stir together flour and baking powder; sprinkle mixture over nuts. Add butter mixture and flour-nut mixture to egg mixture; stir until blended. Spread batter into prepared pan. Bake 35 to 40 minutes or until brownies begin to pull away from sides of pan. Cool in pan on wire rack. Cut into small squares.

Yield: About 30 brownies.

MINI CHIP BROWNIES

½ cup (1 stick) butter
1 cup packed light brown sugar
1 egg
1 teaspoon vanilla extract

1 cup all-purpose flour
½ teaspoon salt
1 cup HERSHEY'S MINI CHIPS
Semi-Sweet Chocolate

Heat oven to 350°F. Grease 8- or 9- inch square baking pan. In small saucepan, melt butter; stir in brown sugar. Remove from heat; pour mixture into small mixer bowl. Cool. Add egg and vanilla; beat well. Add flour and salt; beat just until well blended. Stir in small chocolate chips. Spread batter into prepared pan. Bake 25 to 30 minutes or until brownies begin to pull away from sides of pan. Cool completely in pan on wire rack. Cut into squares.

Yield: 16 brownies.

CHOCOLATE BROWNIES DELUXE

½ cup (1 stick) butter, softened
1 cup sugar
2 eggs
1 teaspoon vanilla extract
1¼ cups all-purpose flour
¼ cup HERSHEY'S Cocoa
¼ teaspoon baking soda
1 cup REESE'S Peanut Butter
  Chips (optional)

¾ cup HERSHEY'S Syrup
Fudge Brownie Frosting:
  3 tablespoons butter, softened
  3 tablespoons HERSHEY'S
  Cocoa
  1 cup powdered sugar
  1 to 2 tablespoons milk
  ¾ teaspoon vanilla extract

Heat oven to 350°F. Grease 13 x 9 x 2-inch baking pan. In large mixer bowl, beat butter, sugar, eggs and vanilla until light and fluffy. Stir together flour, cocoa and baking soda; add alternately with syrup to butter mixture. Stir in peanut butter chips, if desired. Pour batter into prepared pan. Bake 40 to 45 minutes or until brownies begin to pull away from sides of pan. Cool completely in pan on wire rack. Frost with Fudge Brownie Frosting. Cut into bars.

Fudge Brownie Frosting

In small mixer bowl, beat butter and cocoa until blended. Add powdered sugar alternately with milk until of spreading consistency. Stir in vanilla. *About 1 cup frosting.*

Yield: 24 brownies.

CHOCOLATE THUMBPRINT COOKIES

½ cup (1 stick) butter, softened
⅔ cup sugar
1 egg yolk
2 tablespoons milk
1 teaspoon vanilla extract
1 cup all-purpose flour
⅓ cup HERSHEY'S Cocoa
¼ teaspoon salt

Granulated sugar
½ cup pecan or walnut halves
Vanilla Filling:
  ½ cup powdered sugar
  1 tablespoon butter, softened
  2 teaspoons milk
  ¼ teaspoon vanilla extract

In small mixer bowl, beat butter, ⅔ cup sugar, egg yolk, milk and vanilla until light and fluffy. Stir together flour, cocoa and salt; add to butter mixture, beating until well blended. Refrigerate dough at least 1 hour or until firm enough to handle. Heat oven to 350°F. Lightly grease cookie sheet. Shape dough into 1-inch balls; roll in sugar. Place on prepared cookie sheet. Press thumb gently in center of each ball. Bake 10 to 12 minutes or until set. Meanwhile, prepare Vanilla Filling. As soon as cookies are removed from oven, spoon about ¼ teaspoon filling in each thumbprint. Gently press pecan or walnut half in center of each cookie. Carefully remove from cookie sheet to wire rack. Cool completely.

Vanilla Filling

In small bowl, combine powdered sugar, butter, milk and vanilla extract; beat until smooth.

Festive Thumbprint Cookies

For a variation on Chocolate Thumbprint Cookies try this festive version. Dip 1-inch balls of cookie dough into 1 beaten egg white; roll balls in 1 cup chopped nuts or a mixture of 1 cup crushed corn flakes and 2 tablespoons sugar. Bake and fill as directed above. Omit nut half. Gently press unwrapped HERSHEY'S Milk Chocolate Kiss in center of each cookie.

Yield: About 2 dozen cookies.

Thumbprint Cookies; Chocolate Sandwiches (page 95);
Silk Stocking Almond Cookies (page 96)

SILK STOCKING ALMOND COOKIES

½ cup (1 stick) butter or
   margarine, softened
½ cup sugar
½ teaspoon vanilla extract
½ teaspoon almond extract
1 egg
1½ cups all-purpose flour
½ teaspoon salt
½ cup ground almonds

½ cup chopped candied red
   cherries
Chocolate Coating:
   1 cup HERSHEY'S MINI
      CHIPS Semi Sweet Chocolate
   2 HERSHEY'S Milk Chocolate
      Bars (1.55 oz. each), broken
      into pieces
1 tablespoon shortening

In small mixer bowl, beat butter, sugar, vanilla, almond extract and egg until well blended. Gradually add flour and salt; beat until well blended. Stir in almonds and cherries. Divide dough in half; shape each part into an oval-shaped roll, 7 inches long. Wrap each roll in wax paper or plastic wrap; refrigerate 4 to 5 hours or until firm enough to slice. Heat oven to 375°F. Cut dough into ⅛-inch-thick slices. Place on ungreased cookie sheet. Bake 6 to 8 minutes or until lightly browned. Remove from cookie sheet to wire rack. Cool completely. Place wax paper on cookie sheet or tray. Prepare Chocolate Coating. Dip one half of each cookie into coating; place on prepared cookie sheet. Refrigerate until coating is set. Store in cool place.

Chocolate Coating

In top of double boiler, stir together small chocolate chips, chocolate bar pieces and shortening. Place over hot, not boiling, water, stirring occasionally, until chips and chocolate are melted. Remove top of double boiler; set aside until chocolate cools to lukewarm.

Yield: About 5 dozen cookies.

CHOCOLATE SANDWICHES

½ cup (1 stick) butter, softened
1 cup sugar
1 egg
1 teaspoon vanilla extract
1¼ cups all-purpose flour
½ cup HERSHEY'S Cocoa
¾ teaspoon baking soda
¼ teaspoon salt

Creamy Filling:
¼ cup (½ stick) butter,
softened
2½ cups powdered sugar
2 tablespoons milk
1 teaspoon vanilla extract
Red and green food color
(optional)

In large mixer bowl, beat butter, sugar, egg and vanilla until light and fluffy. Stir together flour, cocoa, baking soda and salt; add to butter mixture. Divide dough in half; shape each part into two 1½-inch-thick rolls. Wrap each roll in wax paper or plastic wrap; refrigerate 4 to 5 hours or until firm enough to slice. Heat oven to 375°F. Cut dough into ⅛-inch-thick slices. Place on ungreased cookie sheet. Decorate by drawing tines of fork across each slice. Bake 8 to 10 minutes or until almost firm. Remove from cookie sheet to wire rack. Cool completely. Spread Creamy Filling on flat side of the cookies. Top with remaining cookies, forming sandwiches.

Creamy Filling

In small bowl, beat butter, powdered sugar, milk and vanilla until creamy and of spreading consistency. If desired, divide filling in half; add red food color to one part and green food color to the other part.

Variation: Add strawberry extract to pink filling; mint extract to green filling.

Yield: About 3 dozen sandwich cookies.

CHOCOLATE ALMOND NUGGETS

2 bars (2 oz.) HERSHEY'S
   Unsweetened Baking Chocolate
6 tablespoons butter, softened
1 cup sugar
1 egg
1¾ cups all-purpose flour
2 teaspoons baking powder

Dash salt
½ cup slivered blanched almonds,
   finely chopped
¼ cup milk
Maraschino cherries, quartered, or
   whole blanched almonds

In top of double boiler over hot, not boiling, water melt chocolate; set aside to cool slightly. In large mixer bowl, beat butter and sugar until creamy. Add egg; beat well. Add chocolate; beat until well blended. Stir together flour, baking powder and salt; stir in chopped almonds. Add flour-almond mixture alternately with milk to butter mixture, stirring to blend. Cover dough; refrigerate about 2 hours or until firm enough to handle. Heat oven to 375°F. Shape dough into ¾-inch balls; place on ungreased cookie sheet. Press cherry piece or whole almond in center of each. Bake 8 to 10 minutes or until firm. Remove from cookie sheet to wire rack. Cool completely.

Yield: About 4 dozen cookies.

BLUE RIBBON FRUIT COOKIES

2 bars (2 oz.) HERSHEY'S
   Unsweetened Baking Chocolate
6 tablespoons butter, melted
¾ cup packed light brown sugar
2 eggs
1 cup all-purpose flour
1 teaspoon baking powder

½ teaspoon salt
¼ teaspoon ground cinnamon
½ cup candied pineapple,
   chopped
½ cup chopped nuts
½ cup raisins

Heat oven to 350°F. Lightly grease cookie sheet. In top of double boiler over hot, not boiling, water melt chocolate. In large mixer bowl, beat butter, brown sugar and eggs until well blended. Add chocolate; beat until blended. Stir together flour, baking powder, salt and cinnamon; add to butter mixture, beating until well blended. Stir in pineapple, nuts and raisins. Drop by heaping teaspoonfuls onto prepared cookie sheet. Bake 8 to 10 minutes or until set. Cool slightly; remove from cookie sheet to wire rack. Cool completely.

Yield: About 2 dozen cookies.

Chocolate Fruit Cookies (page 99);
Chocolate Almond Nuggets, Blue Ribbon Fruit Cookies

COCOA BREAD CRUMB COOKIES

¼ cup (½ stick) butter, softened
½ cup sugar
¼ cup HERSHEY'S Cocoa
2 eggs
1 teaspoon vanilla extract
1 cup fine dry bread crumbs

Jam or jelly
Vanilla Frosting:
  2 tablespoons butter, softened
  1¾ cups powdered sugar
  3 to 4 tablespoons milk
  ½ teaspoon vanilla extract

Heat oven to 300°F. Grease 8-inch square baking pan. In small mixer bowl, beat butter and sugar until creamy. Add cocoa; beat until blended. Add eggs and vanilla; beat well. Add bread crumbs; beat until blended. Spread batter into prepared pan. Bake 20 minutes or until wooden pick inserted in center comes out clean. Cool in pan on wire rack. Cut into 1½-inch circles; put two circles together sandwich-fashion with favorite jam or jelly. Frost tops with Vanilla Frosting, allowing some frosting to drizzle down the sides.
  Yield: About 2 dozen 1½ inch filled cookies.

CHOCOLATE FRUIT COOKIES

1 cup shortening
2 cups packed light brown sugar
2 eggs
2 teaspoons baking soda
1 cup milk

3 cups all-purpose flour
½ cup HERSHEY'S Cocoa
1 cup raisins
1 cup chopped walnuts
Vanilla Butter Icing (page 37)

Heat oven to 375°F. Grease cookie sheet. In large mixer bowl, beat shortening and sugar until well blended. Add eggs; beat well. Stir baking soda into milk until dissolved; add to shortening mixture, beating well. Stir together flour and cocoa; gradually add to shortening mixture, beating until well blended. Stir in raisins and walnuts. Drop batter by teaspoonfuls onto prepared cookie sheet. Bake 8 to 10 minutes or until set. Ice with double recipe Vanilla Butter Icing. Add red or green food color to icing, if desired.
  Yield: About 9 dozen cookies.

CHOCOLATE WALNUT WHEELS

2 bars (2 oz.) HERSHEY'S
  Unsweetened Baking Chocolate
⅓ cup butter, softened
1 cup sugar
1 egg
¼ teaspoon vanilla extract

¾ cup all-purpose flour or ⅔ cup
  cake flour
¼ teaspoon salt
1 cup finely chopped walnuts
Walnut halves

Heat oven to 350°F. Lightly grease cookie sheet. In top of double boiler over hot, not boiling, water melt chocolate. Set aside to cool slightly. In large mixer bowl, beat butter and sugar until well blended. Add chocolate, egg and vanilla; beat well. Add flour and salt; beat until blended. Stir in chopped walnuts. Drop by heaping teaspoonfuls onto prepared cookie sheet. Place walnut half in center of each. Bake 10 to 12 minutes or until set. Remove from cookie sheet to wire rack. Cool completely.

Yield: About 2 dozen cookies.

CHOCOLATE DATE AND NUT BARS

2 eggs
½ cup granulated sugar
½ cup all-purpose flour
1 teaspoon baking powder
1 teaspoon vanilla extract

6 tablespoons HERSHEY'S
  Syrup
½ cup dates, chopped
½ cup chopped walnuts
Powdered sugar

Heat oven to 350°F. Grease 9-inch square baking pan. In small mixer bowl, beat eggs. Gradually add granulated sugar, beating until well blended. Stir together flour and baking powder; add to egg mixture, beating until blended. Add syrup and vanilla; beat until blended. Stir in dates and walnuts. Spread batter into prepared pan. Bake 40 minutes or until edges are firm. Cool in pan on wire rack. Cut into 1 x 3-inch bars. Sprinkle powdered sugar over top.

Yield: About 2 dozen bars.

CHOCOLATE PECAN PIE BARS

1⅓ cups all-purpose flour
2 tablespoons plus ½ cup packed
  light brown sugar, divided
½ cup (1 stick) butter
2 eggs
½ cup light corn syrup

¼ cup HERSHEY'S Cocoa
2 tablespoons butter, melted
1 teaspoon vanilla extract
⅛ teaspoon salt
1 cup coarsely chopped pecans

Heat oven to 350°F. In medium bowl, stir together flour and 2 tablespoons brown sugar. Cut in ½ cup butter until mixture resembles coarse crumbs; press onto bottom and about 1 inch up sides of ungreased 9-inch square baking pan. Bake 10 to 12 minutes or until set. With back of spoon, lightly press crust into corners and against sides of pan. Meanwhile, in small bowl, lightly beat eggs, corn syrup, remaining ½ cup brown sugar, cocoa, melted butter, vanilla and salt. Stir in pecans. Pour mixture over warm crust. Return to oven. Bake 25 minutes or until pecan filling is set. Cool in pan on wire rack. Cut into bars.

Yield: 16 bars.

COCOA–MOLASSES DROP CAKES

⅓ cup butter, softened
⅓ cup sugar
⅓ cup molasses
1 egg
¾ cup all-purpose flour

3 tablespoons HERSHEY'S Cocoa
1 teaspoon baking powder
½ cup chopped nuts
Vanilla Drizzle (page 42)

Heat oven to 375°F. In large mixer bowl, beat butter and sugar until blended. Add molasses and egg; beat well. Stir together flour, cocoa and baking powder; add to butter mixture, beating until well blended. Stir in nuts. Drop batter by slightly heaping teaspoonfuls onto ungreased cookie sheet. Bake 6 minutes or until set. Cool slightly; remove from cookie sheet to wire rack. Cool completely. Drizzle Vanilla Drizzle over top of cookies, if desired.

Yield: About 2½ dozen cookies.

MINI CHIP SUGAR COOKIES

⅓ cup butter, softened
¾ cup granulated sugar
½ cup packed light brown sugar
1 egg
1 teaspoon vanilla extract
2 cups all-purpose flour
1 teaspoon baking soda

½ teaspoon baking powder
½ teaspoon salt
½ cup sour milk
2 cups (12 oz. pkg.)
HERSHEY'S MINI CHIPS
Semi-Sweet Chocolate

Heat oven to 350°F. Lightly grease cookie sheet. In large mixer bowl, beat butter, granulated sugar and brown sugar until light and fluffy. Add egg and vanilla; beat well. Stir together flour, baking soda, baking powder and salt; add to butter mixture alternately with sour milk, beating until well blended. Stir in small chocolate chips. Drop batter by heaping teaspoonfuls onto prepared cookie shoot. Bake 8 to 10 minutes or until lightly browned. (Cookies will rise during baking, then flatten.) Remove from cookie sheet to wire rack. Cool completely.

Yield: About 2½ dozen cookies.

Candies

Country Club Two-Story Fudge (page 106),
Chocolate Log Cabin Roll (page 107), Chocolate Pecan Pralines (page 107)

COUNTRY CLUB TWO—STORY FUDGE

First Story:
2¼ cups sugar
1 cup milk
3 bars (3 oz.) HERSHEY'S
  Unsweetened Baking
  Chocolate, broken into pieces
1 tablespoon light corn syrup
2 tablespoons butter
1 teaspoon vanilla extract
½ cup chopped nuts

Second Story:
2½ cups sugar
½ cup light cream
½ cup milk
1 tablespoon light corn syrup
¼ teaspoon salt
2 tablespoons butter
1 teaspoon vanilla extract
⅓ cup chopped candied red
  cherries

First Story

Butter 9-inch square pan; set aside. In heavy 3-quart saucepan, stir together sugar, milk, chocolate pieces and corn syrup. Cook over medium heat, stirring constantly, until chocolate is melted and mixture comes to full, rolling boil. Boil, stirring occasionally, to 234°F or until syrup, when dropped into very cold water, forms a soft ball which flattens when removed from water. (Bulb of candy thermometer should not rest on bottom of saucepan.) Remove from heat. Add butter and vanilla. Do not stir. Cool at room temperature to 110°F (lukewarm). Beat until mixture thickens and starts to lose its gloss; stir in nuts. Quickly spread into prepared pan. Set aside.

Second Story

Butter sides of heavy 2-quart saucepan. In saucepan, stir together sugar, light cream, milk, corn syrup and salt. Cook over medium heat, stirring constantly, until sugar is dissolved and mixture comes to full rolling boil. Boil, without stirring, to 236°F or until syrup, when dropped into very cold water, forms a soft ball which flattens when removed from water. (Bulb of candy thermometer should not rest on bottom of saucepan.) Remove from heat. Add butter and vanilla. Do not stir. Cool at room temperature to 110°F. Beat until fudge thickens and starts to lose its gloss. Quickly stir in cherries. Immediately pour over chocolate fudge. Cool completely. Cut into squares.

Yield: About 4 dozen squares.

CHOCOLATE PECAN PRALINES

1 cup granulated sugar
1 cup packed light brown sugar
½ cup light cream
¼ teaspoon salt
1 tablespoon butter
1 cup coarsely chopped pecans

2 bars (2 oz.) HERSHEY'S
    Unsweetened Baking
    Chocolate, broken into pieces
1 teaspoon vanilla extract

Place wax paper on two cookie sheets; set aside. In heavy large saucepan, stir together granulated sugar, brown sugar, light cream and salt. Cook over medium heat, stirring constantly, to 228°F. (Bulb of candy thermometer should not rest on bottom of saucepan). Remove from heat; add butter, pecans and baking chocolate pieces. Return to heat; cook, stirring constantly, to 234°F or until syrup, when dropped into very cold water, forms a soft ball which flattens when removed from water. Remove from heat; stir in vanilla. Beat 10 to 15 seconds or until slightly thickened. Quickly drop mixture by large spoonfuls onto prepared cookie sheets. Cool until set. Store tightly covered in a cool, dry place.

Yield: About 2 dozen pieces candy.

CHOCOLATE LOG CABIN ROLL

½ cup chopped pecans
1 cup packed light brown sugar
¾ cup granulated sugar
1 cup (½ pt.) light cream
½ cup maple syrup

2 tablespoons butter
1½ bars (1½ oz.) HERSHEY'S
    Unsweetened Baking Chocolate,
    broken into pieces
Dash salt

Butter cookie sheet or another piece wax paper; set aside. Place pecans on wax paper on flat surface. In heavy 3-quart saucepan, combine brown sugar, granulated sugar, light cream, maple syrup, chocolate pieces and salt. Cook over medium heat, stirring constantly, until mixture boils. Cover; cook 5 minutes. Remove cover; boil, stirring occasionally, to 234°F or until syrup, when dropped into very cold water, forms a soft ball which flattens when removed from water. (Bulb of candy thermometer should not rest on bottom of saucepan.) Remove from heat. Do not stir. Cool at room temperature to 110°F (lukewarm). Beat until fudge begins to lose its gloss and holds its shape. Turn out onto prepared cookie sheet. With well-buttered hands, shape into 9-inch roll. Immediately roll in pecans, gently pressing into roll to coat; cut into slices.

Yield: About 18 slices.

CHOCOLATE COCONUT SQUARES

⅓ cup light corn syrup
2 tablespoons sugar
2 tablespoons water
2¼ cups plus 2 tablespoons
   flaked coconut, divided

1 teaspoon vanilla extract
¾ cup HERSHEY'S Semi-Sweet
   Chocolate Chips
⅓ cup toasted slivered almonds
   or chopped pecans

Butter 8-inch square pan; set aside. In small saucepan, stir together corn syrup, sugar and water. Cook to 234°F or until syrup, when dropped into very cold water, forms a soft ball which flattens when removed from water. (Bulb of candy thermometer should not rest on bottom of saucepan.) Remove from heat. Stir in 2¼ cups coconut and vanilla. Pour mixture into prepared pan. In top of double boiler over hot, not boiling, water melt chocolate chips; spread over coconut mixture. Sprinkle almonds and remaining 2 tablespoons coconut over top. Cool. Cut into squares.

Yield: About 3 dozen squares.

CHOCOLATE NUT CLUSTERS

1 cup HERSHEY'S Milk
   Chocolate Chips
1 teaspoon shortening

1 cup cashews, peanuts, broken
   pecans or walnuts

Place wax paper on cookie sheet; set aside. In top of double boiler over hot, not boiling, water melt chocolate chips and shortening. Stir in nuts. Drop nut mixture from fork onto prepared cookie sheet. Refrigerate about 30 minutes or until firm. Store tightly covered in refrigerator.

Yield: About 2½ dozen candies.

ANGEL FUDGE

2 cups sugar
1 cup milk
1 cup HERSHEY'S Syrup

1 tablespoon butter
1 teaspoon vanilla extract
¾ cup marshmallow creme

Butter 8-inch square pan. In heavy 3-quart saucepan, combine sugar, milk and syrup. Cook over medium heat, stirring constantly, until well blended. Continue to cook, without stirring, to 234°F or until syrup, when dropped into very cold water, forms a soft ball which flattens when removed from water. (Bulb of candy thermometer should not rest on bottom of saucepan.) Remove from heat. Add butter, vanilla and marshmallow creme. Do not stir. Cool at room temperature to 110°F (lukewarm). Beat with wooden spoon until fudge loses gloss (fudge will hold shape). Quickly spread into prepared pan; cool. Cut into squares.
Yield: About 3 dozen candies.

FUDGE CARAMELS

2 cups sugar
⅔ cup HERSHEY'S Cocoa
⅛ teaspoon salt
1 cup light corn syrup

1 cup evaporated milk
½ cup water
¼ cup (½ stick) butter
1 teaspoon vanilla extract

Butter 9-inch square pan; set aside. In heavy 4-quart saucepan, combine sugar, cocoa, salt and corn syrup; stir in evaporated milk and water. Cook over medium heat, stirring constantly, until mixture boils. Continue to cook, stirring frequently, to 245°F or until syrup, when dropped into very cold water, forms a firm ball which does not flatten when removed from water. (Bulb of candy thermometer should not rest on bottom of saucepan.) Remove from heat; stir in butter and vanilla, blending well. Quickly pour caramel mixture into prepared pan. When caramel is firm, with buttered scissors, cut into 1-inch squares. Wrap individually in wax paper.
Yield: About 6 dozen candies.

CHOCOLATE PEANUT BUTTER FUDGE

2 cups sugar
3 bars (3 oz.) HERSHEY'S
Unsweetened Baking Chocolate,
broken into pieces

⅔ cup milk
1 cup marshmallow creme
¾ cup peanut butter
1 teaspoon vanilla extract

Butter 9-inch square pan; set aside. In heavy 3-quart saucepan, stir together sugar, milk and chocolate. Cook over medium heat, stirring constantly, until mixture comes to full rolling boil. Boil, without stirring, to 234°F or until syrup, when dropped into very cold water, forms a soft ball which flattens when removed from water. (Bulb of candy thermometer should not rest on bottom of saucepan.) Remove from heat. Add marshmallow creme, peanut butter and vanilla; stir just until blended. Pour into prepared pan; cool. Cut into squares.
Yield: About 3 dozen pieces.

CHOCOLATE TURKISH PASTE

3 envelopes unflavored gelatin
½ cup cold water
2 cups sugar
⅓ cup HERSHEY'S Cocoa

⅔ cup water
1 teaspoon vanilla extract
Sugar

Line bottom of 8-inch square pan with wax paper. In small bowl, sprinkle gelatin over cold water; let stand 10 minutes. In small heavy saucepan, combine 2 cups sugar, cocoa and ⅔ cup water. Cook over medium heat, stirring constantly, until sugar is dissolved. Add gelatin; cook over low heat, stirring until gelatin is completely dissolved and mixture comes to boil. Continue to cook, without stirring, to 220°F. Remove from heat; stir in vanilla. Cool, without stirring, about 30 minutes. Pour mixture into prepared pan. Let stand at room temperature 24 hours. With spatula or knife, loosen edges from sides of pan. Invert onto well-sugared surface. Carefully peel off wax paper; cut into squares. Roll squares in sugar until lightly coated.
Yield: About 4 dozen squares.

CREAMY COCOA TAFFY

1¼ cups sugar
¾ cup light corn syrup
⅓ cup HERSHEY'S Cocoa
⅛ teaspoon salt

2 teaspoons white vinegar
¼ cup evaporated milk
1 tablespoon butter

Butter 9-inch square pan; set aside. In heavy 2-quart saucepan, combine sugar, corn syrup, cocoa, salt and vinegar. Cook over medium heat, stirring constantly, until mixture boils; add evaporated milk and butter. Continue to cook, stirring occasionally, to 248°F or until syrup, when dropped into very cold water, forms a firm ball that does not flatten when removed from water. (Bulb of candy thermometer should not rest on bottom of saucepan.) Pour mixture into prepared pan. Cool until lukewarm and comfortable to handle. Butter hands; immediately stretch taffy, folding and pulling until light in color and hard to pull. Place taffy on table; pull into ½-inch-wide strips (twist two strips together, if desired). With buttered scissors, cut into 1-inch pieces. Wrap individually.

Yield: About 6 dozen pieces or 1¼ pounds.

CHOCOLATE POTATO CANDY

1 medium baking potato
1 teaspoon vanilla extract
½ teaspoon salt

4 cups powdered sugar
⅓ cup HERSHEY'S Cocoa
Chocolate Glaze (page 43)

Place wax paper on cookie sheet; set aside. Bake potato; mash (should yield ¾ cup). In large bowl, combine mashed potato, vanilla and salt. Gradually add powdered sugar and cocoa, beating until mixture is stiff enough to be shaped into 1-inch balls. Refrigerate balls until cold. Dip balls, one at a time, into Chocolate Glaze. Let excess chocolate drip off balls. Place on prepared cookie sheet. Refrigerate until chocolate is set. Store tightly covered in refrigerator.

Yield: About 3 dozen candies.

CHOCOLATE CHIP NOUGAT LOG

3 cups sugar, divided
⅔ cup plus 1¼ cups light corn
  syrup, divided
2 tablespoons water
¼ cup egg whites (about 2 large)
¼ cup butter, melted
2 teaspoons vanilla extract
1 cup HERSHEY'S Semi-Sweet
  Chocolate Chips or
  HERSHEY'S Mini Chips
  Semi-Sweet Chocolate

2 cups chopped walnuts
¼ teaspoon red food color
Walnut halves (optional)
Chocolate Coating (optional):
  1 cup HERSHEY'S Semi-Sweet
    Chocolate Chips or
    HERSHEY'S Mini Chips
    Semi-Sweet Chocolate
  1½ teaspoons shortening (not
    butter or oil)

Line 15½ x 10½ x 1-inch jelly roll pan with foil; butter foil. Set aside. In small saucepan, stir together 1 cup sugar, ⅔ cup corn syrup and water; cook over medium heat, stirring constantly, until sugar dissolves. Cook, without stirring, until mixture reaches 230°F. (Bulb of candy thermometer should not rest on bottom of saucepan.) Continue cooking, but start to beat egg whites. In large mixer bowl, beat egg whites until stiff, but not dry; set aside. Continue cooking, without stirring, to 238°F or until syrup, when dropped into very cold water, forms a soft ball which flattens when removed from water. Remove from heat. Pour hot syrup in a thin stream over egg whites, beating constantly on high speed of a sturdy, freestanding electric mixer, scraping sides of bowl. Continue beating 4 to 5 minutes or until mixture becomes very thick. Cover; set aside. In heavy 2-quart saucepan, combine remaining 2 cups sugar and 1¼ cups corn syrup. Cook over medium heat, stirring constantly, until sugar dissolves. Cook, without stirring, to 275°F or until syrup, when dropped into very cold water, separates into threads that are hard, but not brittle. Pour hot syrup all at once over reserved egg white mixture; blend with wooden spoon. Stir in butter and vanilla. Stir in chopped walnuts. Add food color; stir until well blended. Pour mixture into prepared pan. Sprinkle chocolate chips over top. Cool 6 to 8 hours or until firm. To form into logs, invert pan; remove foil. Cut nougat in half crosswise; roll from cut end, jelly roll style. Spoon Chocolate Coating over logs, if desired. Garnish with walnut halves, if desired. When coating is set, cut logs into ¼-inch slices. Store, well covered, in cool, dry place.

Chocolate Coating

In top of double boiler over hot, not boiling, water melt chips and shortening. Stir until blended.

Yield: About 7 dozen candies.

Chocolate Nougat Log

COCOA RUM BALLS

3 ¼ cups vanilla wafer crumbs
  (12 oz. box vanilla wafers)
¾ cup powdered sugar
¼ cup HERSHEY'S Cocoa

1½ cups chopped nuts
3 tablespoons light corn syrup
½ cup light rum*
Powdered sugar

In large bowl, combine crumbs, ¾ cup powdered sugar, cocoa and nuts. Add corn syrup and rum; blend well. Shape into 1-inch balls and roll in powdered sugar. Store in airtight container 2 to 3 days to develop flavor. Reroll in powdered sugar before serving.

Yield: About 4 dozen balls.

* ½ cup orange juice plus 1 teaspoon grated orange peel can be substituted for rum.

CHOCOLATE COCONUT BALLS

3 bars (3 oz.) HERSHEY'S
  Unsweetened Baking Chocolate
¼ cup (½ stick) butter
½ cup sweetened condensed milk
¾ cup granulated sugar
¼ cup water

1 tablespoon light corn syrup
1 teaspoon vanilla extract
2 cups shredded coconut
1 cup chopped nuts
Powdered sugar

In top of double boiler over hot, not boiling, water melt chocolate and butter. Add sweetened condensed milk; stir to blend. Remove from heat. In small saucepan, stir granulated sugar, water and corn syrup. Cook over medium heat, stirring constantly, until sugar is dissolved. Cook, without stirring, to 250°F or until syrup, when dropped into very cold water, forms a firm ball which does not flatten when removed from water. (Bulb of candy thermometer should not rest on bottom of saucepan.) Remove from heat; stir into chocolate mixture. Add vanilla, coconut and nuts; stir until well blended. Refrigerate about 30 minutes or until firm enough to handle. Shape into 1-inch balls; roll in powdered sugar. Store tightly covered in a cool, dry place.

Yield: About 5 dozen candies.

CHOCOLATE CHIP– PEANUT BUTTER FUDGE

2 cups sugar
²⁄₃ cup milk
2 tablespoons light corn syrup
1 tablespoon butter

1 teaspoon vanilla extract
½ cup peanut butter
½ cup HERSHEY'S Milk
   Chocolate Chips

Butter 8-inch square pan; set aside. In heavy 3-quart saucepan, stir together sugar, milk and corn syrup. Cook over medium heat, stirring constantly, until mixture boils. Continue boiling, without stirring, to 234°F. or until syrup, when dropped into very cold water, forms a soft ball which flattens when removed from water. (Bulb of candy thermometer should not rest on bottom of saucepan.) Remove from heat. Add butter. Do not stir. Cool to 114°F (lukewarm). Add vanilla and peanut butter; beat just until mixture thickens, about 30 seconds. Quickly pour into prepared pan. Immediately sprinkle chocolate chips over top. Cool until firm. Cut into squares.

Yield: About 3 dozen pieces.

CHOCOLATE POPCORN BALLS

8 cups popped popcorn (about
   ⅓ to ½ cup unpopped)
1¼ cups sugar
¾ cup light corn syrup
½ cup HERSHEY'S Cocoa

2 teaspoons cider vinegar
⅛ teaspoon salt
2 tablespoons butter
¼ cup evaporated milk

Remove all unpopped kernels from popped corn. Place popcorn in large bowl; set aside. In heavy 3-quart saucepan, stir together sugar, corn syrup, cocoa, vinegar and salt. Add butter. Cook over medium heat, stirring constantly, until mixture boils. Slowly add evaporated milk, stirring until blended. Continue to cook, stirring occasionally, to 265°F or until syrup, when dropped into very cold water, forms a hard ball when removed from water. (Bulb of candy thermometer should not rest on bottom of saucepan.) Remove from heat; pour mixture over popcorn, stirring gently to coat popcorn. Working quickly, use buttered hands to shape mixture into 2-inch balls. Wrap each ball in clear plastic wrap.

Yield: 10 balls.

Beverages

Orange Chocolate Float (page 122);
Frosted Chocolate Shake (page 120)

FROSTED CHOCOLATE SHAKE

¾ cup milk
2 to 3 tablespoons HERSHEY'S
  Syrup
1 teaspoon sugar

½ teaspoon vanilla extract
½ cup vanilla ice cream
Maraschino cherry (optional)

In blender container, combine milk, syrup, sugar and vanilla; cover and blend. Add ice cream; cover and blend until smooth. Garnish with cherry, if desired. Serve immediately.
Yield: One 10-ounce serving.

CHOCOLATE PINEAPPLE FREEZE

¾ cup pineapple juice
3 tablespoons HERSHEY'S
  Syrup

¼ cup water
Crushed ice

In blender container, combine pineapple juice, syrup and water; cover and blend. Serve immediately over ice.
Yield: One 10-ounce serving.

COCOMOKO FLOAT

½ cup milk
¼ cup cold brewed coffee or ½
  teaspoon powdered instant
  coffee dissolved in ¼ cup
  boiling water

3 tablespoons HERSHEY'S Syrup
2 teaspoons sugar (optional)
½ teaspoon vanilla extract
Crushed ice
Whipped cream

In blender container, combine milk, coffee, syrup, sugar, if desired, and vanilla; cover and blend. Fill glass one-quarter full with ice; add milk mixture. Top with whipped cream. Serve immediately.
Yield: One 8-ounce serving.

RICH ICED CHOCOLATE

4 cups (1 qt.) water
1 cup sugar
4 bars (4 oz.) HERSHEY'S
Unsweetened Baking Chocolate,
  broken into pieces
Dash salt

1 teaspoon vanilla extract
2 cups (1 pt.) cold
  whipping cream
Crushed ice
Whipped cream (optional)

In large saucepan, stir together water and sugar; add chocolate pieces and
salt. Cook over medium heat, stirring occasionally, until mixture comes to
full boil; boil 5 minutes, stirring occasionally. Remove from heat; cool
completely. Stir in vanilla. In large mixer bowl, beat 2 cups whipping cream
until slightly thickened. Add chocolate mixture; beat with rotary beater or
wire whisk until slightly foamy. Fill glasses one-half full with ice; add
chocolate mixture. Top with whipped cream, if desired.

Yield: Eight 8-ounce servings.

Cokomoko Float, Chocolate Pineapple Freeze, Rich Iced Chocolate

HOT COCOA

3 tablespoons sugar
2 tablespoons HERSHEY'S
   Cocoa
Dash salt

¼ cup hot water
1½ cups milk
Marshmallows or marshmallow
   creme

In medium saucepan, combine sugar, cocoa and salt; stir in water. Cook over medium heat, stirring constantly, until mixture boils. Boil and stir 2 minutes. Add milk. Heat to serving temperature, stirring occasionally. Do not boil. Remove from heat; stir in vanilla. Beat with rotary beater or wire whisk until foamy. Serve hot, topped with marshmallows.
   Yield: About three 6-ounce servings.

CHOCOBERRY SPLASH

Crushed Ice
¾ cup cold skim milk
¼ cup sliced fresh strawberries
2 tablespoons vanilla ice milk

2 tablespoons HERSHEY'S
   Syrup
2 tablespoons club soda

Fill tall glass with crushed ice. Into blender container, measure all ingredients except club soda. Cover; blend on medium speed until smooth. Pour into glass over crushed ice; add club soda. Serve immediately.
   Variations: Substitute any of the follow for strawberries: ⅓ cup canned peach slices, drained; 3 tablespoons frozen raspberries, 2 slices or ¼ cup canned pineapple, drained.
   Yield: One 12-ounce serving.

MOCHA SHAKE

¼ cup warm water
2 tablespoons HERSHEY'S
   Cocoa
1 tablespoon sugar

1 cup cold coffee
1 cup vanilla ice cream
Crushed Ice
Whipped cream (optional)

In blender container, combine water, cocoa and sugar. Cover; blend on low speed. Add coffee; cover and blend. Add ice cream; cover and blend until smooth. Serve immediately over crushed ice. Garnish with whipped cream, if desired.
   Yield: About three 6-ounce servings.

CHOCOLATE SYRUP ICED CHOCOLATE

4 cups (1 qt.) cold milk
1½ cups (1-lb.can) HERSHEY'S
  Syrup
1 teaspoon vanilla extract

2 cups (1 pt.) cold whipping
  cream
Whipped cream (optional)

In large pitcher or bowl, stir together milk, syrup and vanilla; set aside. In large mixer bowl, beat 2 cups whipping cream until slightly thickened. Add chocolate mixture; beat with rotary beater or wire whisk until slightly foamy. Fill glasses one-half full with ice; add chocolate mixture. Top with whipped cream, if desired.

Yield: Eight 8-ounce servings.

ORANGE CHOCOLATE FLOAT

½ cup orange juice
2 tablespoons HERSHEY'S
  Syrup
1 tablespoon sugar

Crushed ice
Whipped cream
Orange slice (optional)

In blender container, combine orange juice, syrup and sugar; cover and blend. Pour over ice in glass; top with whipped cream. Garnish with orange slice, if desired. Serve immediately.

Yield: One 6-ounce serving.

HOT COCOA FOR A CROWD

1½ cups sugar
1¼ cups HERSHEY'S Cocoa
½ teaspoon salt

¾ cup hot water
4 quarts (1 gal.) milk
1 tablespoon vanilla extract

In 6-quart saucepan, combine sugar, cocoa and salt; gradually add water. Cook over medium heat, stirring constantly, until mixture boils. Boil and stir 2 minutes. Add milk. Heat to serving temperature, stirring occasionally. Do not boil. Remove from heat; stir in vanilla. Serve hot.

Yield: About 22 6-ounce servings.

FIVE O'CLOCK WHIPPED CHOCOLATE

3 tablespoons sugar
2 tablespoons HERSHEY'S
  Cocoa
Dash salt
¼ cup hot water

1½ cups milk
⅛ teaspoon vanilla extract
2 tablespoons marshmallow
  creme

In medium saucepan, stir together sugar, cocoa and salt; stir in water. Cook over medium heat, stirring constantly, until mixture boils. Boil and stir 2 minutes. Add milk. Heat to serving temperature, stirring occasionally. Do not boil. Remove from heat; stir in vanilla. Beat with rotary beater or wire whisk until foamy. Beat in marshmallow creme. Serve hot.
Yield: Two 8-ounce servings.

SPANISH CHOCOLATE

2 cups (1 pt.) light cream
4 HERSHEY'S Milk Chocolate
  Bars (1.55 oz. each), broken
  into pieces
Whipped cream

¼ cup brewed coffee or ½
  teaspoon powdered instant
  coffee dissolved in ¼ cup
  boiling water

In medium saucepan, combine light cream and chocolate bar pieces. Cook over low heat, stirring constantly, until chocolate is melted and mixture is smooth. Stir in coffee. Beat with rotary beater or wire whisk until foamy. Serve hot with a dollop of whipped cream or cool chocolate mixture and serve cold over crushed ice.
Yield: Five 6-ounce servings.

CHOCOLATE MALTED MILK

1 cup cold milk
3 tablespoons HERSHEY'S
  Syrup

2 to 3 teaspoons malted
  milk powder

In blender container, combine milk, syrup and malted milk powder; cover and blend. Serve immediately.
Yield: One 8-ounce serving.

ROYAL HOT CHOCOLATE

2 bars (2 oz.) HERSHEY'S
    Unsweetened Baking Chocolate
1 can (14 oz.) sweetened
    condensed milk
4 cups boiling water

Dash salt
1 teaspoon vanilla extract
Whipped cream (optional)
Ground cinnamon

In top of double boiler over hot, not boiling, water melt chocolate. Stir in sweetened condensed milk. Gradually add water, stirring until well blended. Stir in salt and vanilla. Serve hot, topped with whipped cream, if desired. Garnish with cinnamon.

Yield: Eight 6-ounce servings.

Royal Hot Chocolate

CHOCOLATE HINTS

■ HERSHEY'S Cocoa may be used in place of unsweetened baking chocolate in most recipes. 3 tablespoons of HERSHEY'S Cocoa plus 1 tablespoon of shortening or oil equals 1 bar (1 oz.) unsweetened baking chocolate.

■ Do not substitute HERSHEY'S Semi-Sweet Chocolate Chips or Milk Chocolate Chips for HERSHEY'S Unsweetened Baking Chocolate.

■ HERSHEY'S baking chocolate products will stay fresh for well over a year if stored in a cool, dry place (60°–70°F).

■ Bloom, the gray film that sometimes appears on chocolate chips and bars, occurs when chocolate is exposed to varying temperatures. It does not affect the taste or quality of the chocolate.

■ Chocolate scorches easily; therefore, melt HERSHEY'S chocolate chips or baking bars in top of double boiler over hot, not boiling, water; stir constantly until melted. Remove from heat. If a double boiler is not available, chocolate may be melted in a heavy saucepan over very low heat while stirring constantly.

■ Measure HERSHEY'S Cocoa by spooning into nested measuring cup; level with metal spatula.

■ HERSHEY'S Cocoa keeps very well when stored at room temperature in the original container. It retains its freshness and quality almost indefinitely without refrigeration. Avoid contact with moisture and/or high heat when storing; they could cause clumping and gray discoloration although neither affect cocoa flavor or quality.

■ Refrigerate HERSHEY'S Syrup after opening. If thinner syrup is desired, place opened can in warm water and stir.

■ Prevent skin from forming on the top of cooked puddings and pie fillings by pressing waxed paper or plastic wrap directly on surface before cooling.

■ Beat hot chocolate beverages with a rotary beater until foamy to prevent formation of a skin on the surface.

■ A wet utensil or the condensation of steam droplets can cause chocolate to get stiff and grainy. If this happens, stir in 1 teaspoon solid vegetable shortening (not butter) for every 2 ounces chocolate.

To sour milk: Use 1 tablespoon white vinegar plus milk to equal 1 cup (1½ teaspoons vinegar plus milk to equal ½ cup). Buttermilk can be used in place of sour milk.